吴永宏◎著

连老外都在用的商务信函大全

一本实用的商务英语信函写作大全

中国纺织出版社有限公司 | 国家一级出版社
全国百佳图书出版单位

图书在版编目（CIP）数据

连老外都在用的商务信函大全／吴永宏著．-- 北京：中国纺织出版社有限公司，2020.12

ISBN 978-7-5180-7931-5

Ⅰ.①连… Ⅱ.①吴… Ⅲ.①商务—英语—信函—写作 Ⅳ.①H315

中国版本图书馆CIP数据核字（2020）第184030号

责任编辑：武洋洋　　责任校对：寇晨晨　　责任印制：储志伟

中国纺织出版社有限公司出版发行

地　址：北京市朝阳区百子湾东里A407号楼　邮政编码：100124

销售电话：010—67004422　传真：010—87155801

http://www.c-textilep.com

中国纺织出版社天猫旗舰店

官方微博 http://weibo.com/2119887771

三河市延风印装有限公司印刷　各地新华书店经销

2020年12月第1版第1次印刷

开　本：880×1230　1／32　印张：8.25

字　数：258千字　定价：45.00元

Preface 前言

也许你精通英语的口语表达，也可以轻松应对各种职场英语考试，但是，你是否一直在苦苦寻找一本书，可以帮你轻松写出得体而又大方的职场E-mail呢？

这本《连老外都在用的商务信函大全》涵盖了商务信函中最常用的12大场景，包括求职、申请、祝贺、业务等最容易遇到的情境，让你从此面对职场E-mail时充满信心。本书收录详细的英文E-mail范本，包括邮件原件和回复，无论是直接套用，还是以自己的风格改写，都能帮你用最简单的方式完成任务，写出一份得体地道的商务信函。

书写职场英语E-mail最重要的就是将要表达的事情或意图以简短而不失礼的方式表达出来。还在担心用词一不小心触犯了外国人的大忌？或者还在担心太礼貌反而讲不清楚事情？这本书将帮你打消所有这些疑虑，随抄随用就是这么简单。

本书内还有独立的二维码，每一个二维码都是相关内容的电子版，手机即可阅览，保存下来即可随时拿来使用。

希望广大读者能通过本书的学习，熟悉职场英语E-mail的写法，同时进一步提升英语写作能力。再多加练习与交流，能真正成为职场达人！

编著者

2020年11月

Contents 目录

Unit 8 祝贺篇

Unit 9 吊唁篇

Unit 10 咨询篇

Unit 11 请求篇

Unit 12 投诉篇

Unit 13 理赔信

Unit 14 道歉篇

Chapter Ⅰ
电子邮件的写法

★ Unit 1 电子邮件的格式
★ Unit 2 电子邮件的注意事项

Unit 1 电子邮件的格式

（1）发件时的电子邮件格式

To（收件人）：输入收件人的电子邮箱地址。

Cc（抄送）：输入接收抄送文件的人的电子邮箱地址，收件人知道此抄送信息。

Bcc（密送）：输入接收抄送文件的人的电子邮箱地址，收件人不知道此抄送信息。

Subject（主题）：输入邮件的简短概括介绍。

Message text area（正文）：输入邮件正文内容。

Attachments（附件）：上传邮件附带的附件文件。

（2）收件时的电子邮件格式

From（发件人）：显示发件人的电子邮箱地址

To（收件人）：显示收件人的电子邮箱地址。

Cc（抄送）：显示接收抄送文件的人的电子邮箱地址。

Date（时间）：显示邮件发送时的时间。

Subject（主题）：显示邮件的简短概括介绍。

Message text area（正文）：显示邮件正文内容。

Attachments（附件）：下载邮件附带的附件文件。

读书笔记

Unit 2 电子邮件的注意事项

1. 邮件一定要有明确的主题，言简意赅，真实反映邮件的内容。千万不要不写主题，或是主题过于冗长、含义不清。
2. 信件结构要完整，称谓和署名不可少，称呼收件人要恰当。开头结尾要有问候语，这样能使邮件读起来更友好。电子邮件中对收信人的称谓，以及开头结尾的问候语与纸本书信的写作原则相同。
3. 根据收件人与自己的熟悉程度、等级关系、邮件的性质等因素，选择恰当的语气进行论述，要时刻站在收件人的立场上考虑。
4. 正文内容要简明扼要，行文通顺，最好能在一封邮件中将全部相关信息传达清楚、准确。若事情复杂，可分段列表进行说明，并保持段落的简洁干练。也可采用倒金字塔式的写作方式，先写重要内容，随着叙述的展开，重要性逐渐减弱。这种方式可以在有限的版面内尽快将信息传达给收件人。
5. 如果邮件带有附件，应在正文里提示收件人查看附件，并简要介绍附件内容。附件若是特殊格式文件，也要在正文中说明打开方式。附件文件的命名要让收件人一目了然，附件数目较多时应压缩打包再发送。
6. 收到他人邮件后应及时回复，理想的回复时间是两小时内。若事情复杂，不能确切回复，至少也应该及时回复收到，说明正在处理中。

读书笔记

读书笔记

Chapter Ⅱ

电子邮件的范文

Unit 3 求职篇

（1）如何写

求职类邮件非常重要，一封好的求职信能够给HR留下深刻印象，进而能够帮求职者赢得面试机会。撰写该类邮件时应该注意做到以下几个方面：

a）写明写信人的地址、写信日期和收信人的姓名、地址。

b）文章称呼要正规，如果知道对方姓名，要有尊称；如果不知道收信方是谁，则一般要用“尊敬的领导”。

c）第一段要表明自己写信的目的、应聘的岗位及职位信息来源，态度要诚恳友善。第二段说明自己的能力和优势，特别要针对自己所要申请岗位的要求。应届毕业生可以强调自己的学习成绩、担任职务和实习经验，有工作经验者还要强调工作经验。第三段表现自己的强烈意愿和希望，恳请招聘方给予面试机会，并让招聘方相信自己的决心。

d）文章最后切记要写上自己的联系方式，便于招聘方联系。最后表达美好的祝愿。

e）一般的求职信都会附加简历，来帮助招聘者更好地了解应聘者的素质和能力。因此，附简历的话要注明。

（2）实用例句

a）I am writing to apply for the job that you post on the Internet.

我想要申请你们在网上发布的招聘职位。

b）I am very pleased to introduce myself to you and wish to apply for the job that...

我很高兴在这里介绍自己，我希望能够申请这个职位……

c）I was told that your company needs an executive secretary, and I am so happy to introduce myself to you that I...

我得知贵公司要招聘一名行政秘书，很高兴能在这里介绍自己……

d) I have a good education background which provides me with a good knowledge about the job.

我拥有良好的教育背景，让我对这个工作有很好的认识和了解。

e) I think I am very suitable for your company. I hope you can provide me with opportunities for employment.

我觉得自己非常适合在你们公司发展。希望你们能够为我提供就业的机会。

f) I am looking forward to working with you to discuss about design issues as well as my career planning. Hope you can give me the chance to have a face-to-face interview.

我期待能与您讨论关于设计方面的问题以及自己的职业生涯规划。希望能给我这次面对面探讨的机会。

g) I am skilled in communication, and good at leading and market analysis. You can see the specific information in my resume.

我具有很强的沟通能力、领导能力以及市场分析的能力。具体的信息你可以在我的简历中看到。

h) I think the interview yesterday was very flexible which asked a high level of interview skills. So I want to know more about my interview.

我觉得昨天的面试非常灵活，对我们的面试技巧要求比较高。这样我就更想知道我的面试成绩。

i) I am looking forward to your reply. Thank you so much for your help.

我很期待您的回复，非常感谢您的帮忙。

j) If it is convenient for you, could you help me check my interview result? And then tell me the result. So I can prepare early, to find another job.

如果方便的话，能不能帮我查一下我的面试成绩，告诉我面试的结果？这样我可以早做准备，找其他的工作。

范例 1｜询问职缺

Dear Mr. Henry,

I am a designer who has a four-year experience of designing. And I have worked for a lot of companies as a senior designer. I know your company is one of China's best design companies, so I want to consult if your company needs a designer.

I know this job needs strong professional knowledge. I have a master's degree in graphic design, and some of my works have won awards. What's more, I have a strong sense of responsibility, executive ability and a good team spirit. I am able to work under high pressure and strength.

I am looking forward to working with you to discuss about design issues as well as my career planning. Hope you can give me the chance to have a face-to-face interview. My telephone number is 534-364-4223. Thank you in advance for your help.

Yours sincerely,

George

尊敬的亨利先生：

我是一个有四年工作经验的设计师，曾经在很多公司担任高级设计师一职。我知道你们公司在设计方面非常出色，在全国名列前茅。所以我想要咨询一下，你们公司是否需要招聘设计师。

我知道这项工作需要很强的专业知识，我有平面设计专业的硕士学位，我的一些作品也获得过奖项。同时我有很强的责任感和执行力，有很好的团队精神，能够在较大的压力和强度下工作。

我期待能与您讨论关于设计方面的问题以及自己的职业生涯规划。希望能给我这次面对面探讨的机会。我的联系电话是534—364—4223。提前在这里感谢您的帮助。

乔治 谨上

读书笔记

邮件回复 *Reply*

Dear George,

Recently many departments of our company are hiring employees, including the human resources department, marketing department, financial department and the design department. There are many positions you can choose. But first of all, please send your resume and application letter to me. Then we will inform you of the specific interview time and place. Based on your good design foundation and experience, I think you can go to apply for the design department.

Good luck!

Yours sincerely,

Henry

亲爱的乔治：

我们公司最近有很多部门在招聘人员，主要包括人力资源部、营销部、财务部及设计部。有很多职位可以供你选择。但是首先，请你把你的简历和求职信发给我。然后我们会通知你具体的面试时间和地点。基于你有良好的设计基础和经验，我认为你可以去应聘设计部。

祝好！

亨利 谨上

邮件回复 *Reply*

Dear George,

Recently many departments of our company will hire new staffs. But unfortunately, our design department has not a plan to recruit new employees. If you would like to apply for a job in our company, I suggest you take interviews of other departments, and then when the design department has any vacancy you can transfer to the design work. If you have other better choices, then wish you good luck.

Yours sincerely,

Henry

亲爱的乔治：

最近我们公司的很多部门都会招聘，但是很抱歉，我们的设计部没有招聘意向。如果你愿意的话，我建议你先去别的部门面试，到时候设计部有空缺再调到设计部工作。如果你还有其他更好的选择，那么祝你好运。

亨利 谨上

范例 2 | 求职

Dear Sir or Madam:

I noticed your advertisement for the services of an administrative assistant in last morning's newspaper. I beg to offer myself for the position, feeling confident that I am qualified to fill it to your satisfaction.

I am twenty five years of age, and unmarried. Having graduated from a commercial school two years ago, I was in YYT Company for a year, where I filled a situation similar to that indicated by you.

Should my application be regarded favorably, I shall endeavor to justify the confidence you may repose in me.

Yours faithfully,

Zhang Ying

亲爱的先生/女士：

我在昨天早晨的报纸上读到贵公司正在招聘行政助理的消息。我认为自己能够胜任这一职位，并且能让你们感到满意，特此申请。

我25岁，未婚。两年前从一所商业学校毕业，之后进入YYT公司工作了一年，我的岗位与贵公司招聘岗位相似。

如果贵公司能够接受我的申请，我将会努力工作，不辜负你们对我的信心。

张英 敬上

邮件回复 *Reply*

Dear Miss Zhang,

Thank you for your application for the position of an administrative assistant.

We regret to inform you that the position has been filled. However, we will keep your application on file so that we can contact you when this is a vacancy in the future.

Thank you again for your interest in our company.

Yours Sincerely,

ABC Company

亲爱的张小姐：

感谢你申请我公司行政助理一职。

我们很抱歉地通知你该职位已经招满。然而，我们会将你的简历存档，这样将来我们有空缺的时候会再与你联系。

再一次感谢你对本公司的兴趣。

ABC公司 谨上

范例 3 | 求职自荐

Dear Sir or Madam:

I am replying to your advertisement in the March 23 edition of *Wuhan Evening*.

As indicated in my resume, I have had two-year's experience of keeping accounts for BBC Company. In this position, I was responsible for book keeping, vouchers preparation and filings. I have been good at reporting and commenting on financial performance.

Because it is difficult to indicate every area of my expertise in the resume, I would appreciate the opportunity to meet with you to discuss my qualifications for this position.

I look forward to meeting you.

Yours sincerely,

Wang Yong

尊敬的先生/女士：

我看到3月23日武汉晚报上贵公司刊登的招聘广告，特此应征。

正如我的简历中描述的那样，我在BBC公司做过两年会计。我的岗位职责是记账、凭证编制以及归档。我擅长报告财务数字和对财务表现进行评价。

由于简历不能全面展示我的能力，我很期待有机会能够和您面谈，以证明我适合这一职位。

期待与您见面。

王永 敬上

邮件回复 *Reply*

Dear Mr. Wang,

Thank you for applying for our company's position.

We are pleased to announce that your application for thc position as an accountant has been accepted, and we would like you to come for an interview.

We are pleased to arrange an appointment for you to speak with Mr. Jones, director of the Personnel, at 10:00 a.m. on April 5.

Yours sincerely,

ABC Corporation

亲爱的王先生：

非常感谢您应征我们公司的职位。

我们很荣幸通知您我们接受您应征会计一职的申请，并且希望您来进行面试。

我们很高兴安排您与我公司人事部经理琼斯先生面谈，时间为4月5日上午10点。

ABC公司 谨上

范例 4 | 求职推荐

Dear Sir,

When Tom Smith handed me his resignation, I was, of course, sorry to learn that one of our top salesmen would be leaving. But at the same time, I am willing to say a kind word on his behalf.

Tom has worked for our company for about five years, responsible for developing Hubei and the surrounding area. He has been quite successful in achieving and even surpassing all of his annual sales targets. He has won appreciation and respect from his supervisors and colleagues through his hard work and great efforts. His superior intelligence and good sense of responsibility impressed everyone who had dealings with him.

It is my great honor to recommend a promising young man like Tom and I believe he will more than meet your expectations.

Yours sincerely,

Allen Liu

BBC Company

尊敬的先生：

当汤姆·史密斯向我递交辞呈时，当得知我们最出色的推销员之一将离开我们的时候，我当然感到很遗憾。但是，我仍很愿意为他说句好话。

汤姆已经为我们公司服务了近五年，负责湖北及周边地区的市场开拓。他一直成功地完成甚至超越每年的销售目标。他以自己的努力和勤奋赢得了上司和同事的赏识和尊重。他智慧过人，责任感强，给每个与他有过交往的人都留下了深刻的印象。

我很荣幸推荐这样一位前途光明的年轻人，并且相信他会比你们预想的更优秀。

BBC公司 艾伦刘 敬上

邮件回复 *Reply*

Dear Mr. Liu,

Thank you for your letter, recommending Mr. Smith. As you have mentioned, we were impressed by his intelligence, eloquence and good sense of humor.

Yours sincerely,

ABC Company

尊敬的刘先生，

感谢您来函推荐史密斯先生。正如您所提到的史密斯先生的睿智、口才及幽默感给我们留下了深刻的印象。

ABC公司 敬上

范例 5 | 推荐人确认

Dear Mr. Huang,

Thank your for your reference letter written for Mr. Zhang Hua to facilitate his application for the position of store manager in our company.

Attached please find a copy of the reference letter that we have received. If you would like to provide us with any additional information about the candidate, please contact us by fax: 027-84115133 or by email: rsc@whgy.com.cn .

Thank you.

Yours sincerely,

GGT Company

亲爱的黄先生：

感谢您为张华先生应征敝公司库管经理一职所写的推荐信。

附件请查收我们收到的推荐信复印件一份。如果您对此应征者还有未尽的情况向我们提供，请以传真(027-84115133)或电邮（rsc@whgy.com.cn）的形式与我们联系。

感谢您！

GGT公司 敬上

邮件回复 *Reply*

Dear Sir,

I acknowledge receipt of your letter of March 10, 2019, enclosing a copy of my recommendation for Zhang Hua.

As I have mentioned in the reference letter, Mr. Zhang was always punctual, hard-working and ready to take on new responsibilities. Hc has developed into a resourceful and result-oriented store keeper who, I believe, will be a good asset to your company.

Yours sincerely,

Huang Yilong

FOB Company

亲爱的先生：

我收了您2019年3月10日的信及附件中我为张华所写的一封推荐信。

正如我在推荐信中所提到的，张先生向来不迟到早退，工作勤勤恳恳，并且愿意承担新的任务。他是一个经验丰富，注重结果的库管员。我相信他会成为你公司的栋梁之材。

FOB公司

黄一龙 敬上

范例 6 | 请求安排面试

Dear Sir or Madam:

I have sent you by E-mail a resume to apply for the position of a sales assistant in your company. But, unfortunately, I have not gotten any reply from you. I have to assume that you are so busy that you have neglected it.

My name is Zhang Lin, a newly graduate from Nanjing University, majoring in marketing and obtaining my bachelor's degree with honor. I completed my internship program in BBC companying with good performance. And I believe I am qualified to fill the position you advertised for.

I sincerely hope that you can arrange an interview to discuss about my qualification. I am available for it at your convenience.

Yours sincerely,

Zhang Lin

亲爱的先生/女士：

我通过电邮向你们发送了一份简历，应征贵公司销售助理一职。但遗憾的是，我一直没有收到回复。我只能认为你们太忙以至忽略了。

我叫张林，刚刚从南京大学毕业。我的专业是市场营销，以优异的成绩获得学士学位。我在BBC公司实习过，表现良好。我相信我能够胜任你们招聘的职位。

我真诚地希望你们能够为我安排一次面试，来考核我是否合格。只要你们方便，我任何时候都能参加面试。

张林 敬上

邮件回复 *Reply*

Dear Mr. Zhang,

We have received your resume and your letter of March 28, asking for an interview. We are sorry we were unable to reply your letters in time because of the heavy work load.

We take pleasure to inform that we accept your initial application and we are looking forward to meeting you at 10:00 a.m. on April 2, 2019.

Yours sincerely,

ABC Company

亲爱的张先生：

我们已经收到了你的简历，及你3月28请求面试的来信。我们很抱歉由于工作繁忙没能及时给你回复。

我们很高兴地通知你我们接受你初步的申请，并且期待2019年4月2日上午10点与你面谈。

ABC公司 谨上

范例 7 | 询问面试结果

Dear Mr. Toffler,

I am writing this letter to inquire about my interview. I was lucky to have an interview in your company last Saturday. I hope that I can enter your company through this interview.

The position I applied for is the secretary of the general manager. And the time of the interview was last Saturday, September 4th at 10:00 in the morning. My name is Tom Cook. I think my performance in the interview is good, so I feel quite confident of this interview.By now I still have not received any notice, so I want to write this letter to ask the result.

I appreciate your time to read this letter. I am looking forward to your reply.

Good luck!

Yours sincerely,

Tom

尊敬的托夫勒先生：

我写这封信的目的是为了询问一下我的面试结果。我很幸运上周六在你们公司进行了一场面试。我非常希望能够通过这个面试进入你们公司。

我面试的职位是总经理秘书。面试的时间是在上周六，9月4日上午10点，我的名字叫汤姆·库克。我觉得自己在面试中的表现还可以，对自己还是蛮有信心的。但是还没有收到任何通知，所以我想写信询问一下。

非常感谢你能够在百忙中阅读这封信。我期待您的回信。

祝好！

汤姆 谨上

邮件回复 *Reply*

Dear Tom,

I'm glad you take this interview so seriously. I checked the interview transcripts, and found your grades were very good, ranking the second. Congratulations! You are admitted by our company. We will send the admission notice on this Wednesday. Please pay attention to it.

Yours sincerely,

Toffler

亲爱的汤姆：

我很高兴你对这个面试这么重视。我查了一下面试成绩单，发现你的成绩非常的好，排在第二位。恭喜你！你被我们公司录取了。我们正式的录取通知书将会在这周三发出。请注意查收。

托夫勒 谨上

范例 8 | 感谢给予职位

Dear Mr. Liu,

As we discussed on the phone, I am very pleased to accept the position of marketing manager in PPT Company. Thank you for the opportunity. I am eager to make a positive contribution to the company and to work with everyone there.

As we discussed, my starting salary will be ¥3,000, and insurance and housing fund benefits will be provided after 3 months of employment.

I look forward to starting employment on April 20, 2020. If there is any additional information or paperwork you need prior to then, please let me know.

I, again, extend my sincere gratitude to you.

Yours sincerely,

Zhang Lin

尊敬的刘先生，

正如我们电话中谈到的，我很高兴接受PPT公司提供的营销经理一职。感谢您提供给我这一机会。我期待着能为贵公司做出积极的贡献，并且能和贵公司的职员一起共事。

我们讨论过，我的起薪是3000元，3个月后办理五险一金。

我期待2020年4月20日报到上班。如果在那之前，还需要其他信息或材料，请与我联系。

再次表示感谢。

张林 敬上

邮件回复 *Reply*

Dear Mr. Zhang,

We acknowledge your mail of April 14, accepting the position of marketing manager.

We are looking forward to your arrival on April 20, 2020.

If you need any help, please do not hesitate to tell us.

Yours sincerely,

PPT Company

亲爱的张先生，

我们收到了你4月14日的邮件，并且表示愿意接受你担任营销经理一职。

我们期待你2020年4月20日来报到。

如果有什么需要，请不要犹豫，尽管告知我们。

PPT公司 谨上

范例 9 | 拒绝工作邀请

Dear Mr. Clinton,

I'm pleased to receive your letter to tell me I had been accepted by your company. This is good news for me. I like your company. But I'm sorry that I have to refuse this offer, because I had received a notice of acceptance from New York University. I decided to go to my ideal university to continue my study. I'm sorry to let you down and I hope next time I can have the chance to enter the company.

Best wishes!

Yours sincerely,

Liu Ming

尊敬的克林顿先生：

我很高兴收到你的来信告知我已经被你们公司录取了。这对我来说是个非常棒的消息。我很喜欢你们的公司。但是我很遗憾我必须拒绝这个录取。因为我已经收到纽约大学的录取通知书。我决定去我理想的大学继续学习。很抱歉让您失望。希望下次我还能有机会进入你们公司。

祝好！

刘明 谨上

邮件回复 *Reply*

Dear Liu Ming,

I'm glad to hear that you had received the offer of the New York University. We all think you are a great talent. I hope you can return to our company after you finish your study. You are welcomed to our company.

Wish you all the best.

Yours sincerely,

Clinton

亲爱的刘明：

我很高兴听到你被纽约大学录取的消息。我们都认为你是个很棒的人才。希望你学成归来可以来我们公司。我们非常欢迎你加入我们。

祝你一切顺利。

克林顿 谨上

范例 10 | 拒绝求职者

Dear Liu Ming,

I am so happy to hear from you. I think you are a thoughtful person. I appreciate your courage and determination. Thank you for your attention to our company. But I am sorry to tell you that you are not accepted by our company, because this job asks for about at least five years' work experience about designing. I think you will have the chance next time. Please keep trying.

Best wishes!

Yours sincerely,

Clinton

亲爱的刘明：

我很高兴收到你的来信。我认为你是个很有思想的人。我很欣赏你的勇气和决心。谢谢你对我们公司的关注。但是我很抱歉，我们不能录取你，因为我们这个工作要求有至少五年以上设计相关的经验。但是我想下次你会有机会的。继续努力。

祝好！

克林顿 谨上

邮件回复 *Reply*

Dear Mr. Clinton,

Thank you for your letter. I was frustrated after receiving this letter, because I really like the working environment and atmosphere of your company. Therefore I spent a lot of energy and time on the interview. Work experience is very important, but I think thought is more important. I will continue to fight for my dream.

Best wishes!

Yours sincerely,

Liu Ming

尊敬的克林顿先生：

谢谢你的来信。知道这个消息以后，我很沮丧。因为我真的很喜欢你们公司的工作环境和氛围。为了这次面试我付出了很多精力和时间。工作经验很重要，但是我认为思想更重要。我会继续为我的理想奋斗。

祝好！

刘明 谨上

范例 11 | 辞职

Dear Mr. Stephen,

With this letter I officially submit my resignation that I will resign the position as the assistant of general manager. I will leave the company on 10th next month. Hope you can make the arrangements.

The reason of my leaving is that my father is badly ill. He was diagnosed with cancer. I need to take care of him for a long time. And I want to concentrate on taking care of him. Thank you very much for training me for two years, and colleagues also help me a lot. During this period I have learned much knowledge and many skills, which will benefit me in future days. I'm very grateful.

Before I leave, I will make the rest of the work clear to my colleagues. Try not to delay the work progress. If you have any questions, I am willing to provide help any time.

Best wishes!

Yours sincerely,

Abby

尊敬的斯蒂芬先生：

在此，我将正式辞去我总经理助理的职位。我将在下个月10号正式离职。希望你能够做出些安排。

我离职是为了照顾我重病的爸爸。他被查出患了癌症，需要家人长时间的照顾。所以，我想专心在家照顾老人。非常感谢这两年来公司对我的培养，以及同事们对我的帮助。我在这段时间里学会了很多的知识和技能，这将会有利于我以后的发展。所以我很感激。

在离职前，我会向同事们交代好剩下的工作。尽量不耽误工作的进展。如果有任何问题，我愿意随时提供帮助。

祝好！

艾比 谨上

读书笔记

邮件回复 Reply

Dear Abby,

We have received your letter. I'm sorry that we will lose such a good employee. During these two years, you are excellent in your job and bring a lot of achievements to our company. Now that you have the reason that you must leave, we understand that. We will arrange the work as soon as possible.

Best wishes!

Yours sincerely,

Stephen

亲爱的艾比：

你的来信我已经收到。我很遗憾，我们将失去你这样一位优秀的员工。你在这两年的时间里，工作非常的出色，给公司带来了很多的业绩。既然你已经说明了要离职的理由，我们表示理解。我们会尽快安排好工作。

祝好！

史蒂芬 谨上

读书笔记

范例 12 | 解雇

Dear Mr. Li,

We will terminate your employment on Tuesday, 7 December, because your mistake in the work has brought a great loss to the company. The company needs to pay 100,000 yuan to the customer because of your mistake. After discussion about this, we decide to terminate your employment.

Before you leave please finish the project you are working on. Then return the employee access badge and other property of the company. You will be paid until that day. And your paycheck will be mailed to you.

You have the right to formally appeal your termination within one week after receiving this letter. If you have any questions, please contact me.

Sincerely,

George

尊敬的李先生：

我们将会在12月7日，周二结束你与本公司的聘约。因为你工作的失误给公司造成很大的损失。因为你的失误公司需要支付给顾客100000元的赔偿。我们经过讨论，决定终止与你的聘约。

在你离开之前，请你完成好手上的项目。然后归还公司的员工进出证及其他的公司财产。你的工资将会结算到那天，工资支票将会邮寄给你。

你有权在收到解雇信一周内提出诉讼。如果你有任何问题，请联系我。

乔治 谨上

邮件回复 *Reply*

Dear George,

I am so sad to receive this letter. I know I have made a big mistake and caused a big problem. I feel really sorry for this. I will finish the project before the deadline and return the property of the company.

Sincerely,

Li Hua

亲爱的乔治：

收到这封信我很伤心。我知道我犯了个很大的错误，引起了很大的问题。我感到非常的抱歉。我将会在截止日期前完成我手上的项目，归还公司的物品。

李华 谨上

Unit 4 申请篇

（1）如何写

a）说明自己写信的目的，即清楚地说明自己的申请要求；

b）写明申请的原因以及自己符合申请的条件，并希望对方能够答应；

c）表达对对方的祝福和感谢。

（2）实用例句

a）I hope you can give me this opportunity. Thank you very much.

希望您能给我这次机会，非常感谢。

b）I am writing this letter in order to apply for working in a different department.

我写这封信的目的是为了申请调换部门。

c）I'd like to apply for the staff dormitory. I hope this application can be approved.

我想要申请员工宿舍。希望能够批准。

d）Because of the bad cold, I can't come to work and I want to have a day off to rest at home. Tomorrow I will go to work on time. I hope you can agree. Thank you!

因为重感冒，今天没办法来上班，想要请一天假在家休息。明天我会准时上班。希望您能准假，谢谢！

e）A few days ago I read a notice which said the company was providing the opportunity of in-service training. I really want to apply for the quota.

前几天我看到通知说公司在提供在职进修的机会。我非常想要申请这个名额。

f）I believe that interest is the best teacher. As long as I keep learning and accumulating work experience, I will do a better job. I hope you can consider my request. Thank you!

我相信兴趣是最好的老师，只要我不断地学习，累积经验，我会把工作做得更好。希望您能考虑我的请求。谢谢！

g）So I am writing to apply for a new fax machine as soon as possible. I hope you can agree with this application.

所以我们想要申请尽快购买一台新的传真机。希望您能批准。

h）Thank you for your consideration. I hope I can receive good news from you.

谢谢您的考虑。我希望能听到好消息。

i）I have a strong ability of learning and I am also innovative. So I believe I can excellently do this job.

我有很强的学习能力和创新力，所以我相信我会很出色地做好这个工作。

j）Please approve my application. I am so appreciating that.

请批准我的申请。非常感激。

读书笔记

范例 1 | 求职申请

Dear Sir,

I have learned from the *Want column of the China Post* that you have a vacancy for an English editor, and I am extremely interested in the position.

I have worked for the White Publishing House for 4 years and I am primarily responsible for book editing. My performance has been acknowledged by my superiors and a large number of readers. But that place is quite far away from my home and I really want to work in your company so that I can get close to my family.

I am looking forward to hearing from you!

Enclosed please find my resume.

Yours sincerely,

Maggie

尊敬的先生：

我从《中国邮报》招聘版上得知贵公司正在招聘一名英语编辑，我对这一职位非常感兴趣。

我为怀特出版社工作了4年，主要负责图书编辑。我的工作得到了上司和广大读者的好评。但是那家出版社距离我家太远，我希望能进入贵公司工作，这样能离家人更近一些。

期待您的电话！

随信附上我的简历。

玛吉 敬上

邮件回复 *Reply*

Dear Maggie,

We are writing to acknowledge your application letter as well as your resume. We have studied your resume and want to have a face-to-face talk with you to make our final decision. Will you be able to come to our company this Friday afternoon with your recent photo?

We are looking forward to meeting you!

Yours sincerely,

ABC Company

亲爱的玛吉：

我们收到了您的求职信及简历。经研究，我们觉得还需要和您进行面对面的洽谈才能做出最后的决定。本周五下午您能带上您的个人近照到我们公司来一趟吗？如能到访，请携带一张个人近照。

期待与您的会面！

ABC公司 谨上

范例 2 | 请假申请

Dear Mr. Lin,

I would like to know if I could ask for a casual leave of absence for one day on May 14th, this Wednesday.

This morning I received a telephone call from my dentist, urging me to come to his practice for immediate treatment of my teeth. I have been experiencing a stinging pain, depriving me of my sleep during the past fortnight. The situation could worsen, should infection occur.

Concerning my workload, as Wednesday is not as busy as the other weekdays, I think a one-day leave this Wednesday may be the best solution. I apologize for the inconvenience my absence from work may cause.

Thank you for your understanding. I will call you at 1:30 p.m. or you can call me at any time.

Yours sincerely,

Mary

尊敬的林先生：

我想要在5月14日即本周三请一天事假。

今天早晨我的牙医给我打电话，通知我尽早去他的诊所做牙齿治疗。过去的两周，我牙疼得厉害，无法入眠。要是发生感染，情况可能更糟。

考虑到我的工作情况（周三没有那么忙），我想周三请假一天是最好的选择。由于我的缺勤可能造成的不便，我深表歉意。

感谢您的理解。我会在午间1点半给您打电话，或者您也可以随时打给我。

玛丽 敬上

邮件回复 *Reply*

Dear Mary,

I am very sorry to hear that you have suffered from a toothache. Don't worry about your work. I will ask Linda to deal with your case while you are absent. Please take good care of yourself and call me if you need any help.

Wish you recover soon.

Yours sincerely,

Lin Tao

亲爱的玛丽：

听到你牙疼难忍的消息，我很抱歉。不要担心工作。你不在的时候，我会让琳达帮忙处理你的事务。照顾好自己，有什么需要就给我打电话。

祝你早日康复！

林涛 谨上

范例 3 | 信用证申请

Dear Sir,

Thank you for your mail of March 15, containing your acceptance of our offer for 400 Model PT-250 typewriters.

We ask that you promptly open an irrevocable L/C in our favor, valid until April 2.

Upon receiving your L/C, we will promptly complete shipment arrangements of your order. We will of course, notify you when we have completed the shipment.

We are looking forward to your early and favorable reply.

Yours sincerely,

BOT Company

尊敬的先生：

感谢贵方3月15日来信表示接受我方对400台PT-250型号打字机的报价。

我方请你方立即以我方为受益人开具不可撤销信用证，有效期到4月2日。

我方收到你方的信用证就会立即安排装运你方订单货物。我方定会通知你方完成装运的时间。

我方期待你方尽早回复。

BOT公司 敬上

邮件回复 *Reply*

Dear Sir,

Thank you for your mail of March 16. Complying with your request for opening an irrevocable L/C, we have instructed Industrial and Commercial Bank of China to open a credit for ￥100,000 in your favor, valid until April 2. Please inform us when the order is executed.

Thank you for your cooperation.

Yours sincerely,

ABC Company

尊敬的先生：

非常感谢贵方3月16日的来信。根据你方开立不可撤销信用证的要求，我方已经通知中国工商银行开立金额为 100000元人民币的信用证，你方为受益人，有效期至4 月 2 日。你方执行订单时，请告知我方。

感谢您的合作！

ABC公司 谨上

范例 4 | 商标注册申请

Dear Director of Patents and Trademarks,

ABC Company

Hubei

12 Lianhu Road, Hanyang District, Wuhan

The above identified applicant has been adopted and is using the trademark shown in the accompanying drawing for Weijie washing machine and requests that such mark be registered in the Patent and Trademark Bureau of P.R.China on the Principal Register established by the Act of Patent and Trademark.

The trademark was first used on the goods on January 10, 2011; and it has been in use by now. The mark is used by applying it to labels affixed to the product. Five specimens showing the mark as actually used are presented here.

ABC Company

尊敬的专利商标局局长：

ABC公司

湖北

武汉市汉阳区莲湖路12号

上述申请人已经并正将附图中展示的商标用于卫洁洗衣机，现请求中国专利商标局在依我国专利商标法建立的商标目录上对该商标予以注册。

该商标于2011年1月10日第一次用于该商品，且现在仍在使用。该商标用于产品上的附标签。现附上 5 份样品，显示商标的实际使用情况。

ABC公司

邮件回复 *Reply*

ABC Company:

We acknowledge receipt of your application, asking for registration of the trademark for your Weijie washing machine. We will deal with it as soon as possible and you can expect our approval in about five week days.

Patent and Trademark Bureau of P.R.C

ABC公司：

我们收到了你公司的申请，要求注册你公司卫洁洗衣机的商标。我们会尽快处理，你们在5个工作日内会收到我们的批复。

中华人民共和国专利商标局

范例 5 | 许可证申请

Dear President of Pala,

I, Li Min, do hereby apply for a license to show the trademark of your corporation, "Pala", at my place of business situated at 18 Lotus Lake Road, in Wuhan.

This application accords with the franchising regulations of your corporation. I know more about the regulations that govern the display of the said trademark and the manner of conducting business, and I agree to follow up such regulations at all times.

Yours sincerely,

Li Min

尊敬的派乐集团总裁：

本人，李敏，特此郑重申请贵公司商标使用许可证，因此我位于武汉市莲湖路18号的店面便可以获准使用“派乐”商标。

本申请系依据贵公司加盟条例提出。本人清楚贵公司对上述商标使用和业务经营模式的规范条例，并且同意永久遵守这些条例。

李敏 敬上

邮件回复 *Reply*

Dear Ms. Li,

Through the examination of our company, we strongly feel that there is both a professional and personal fit between you and Pala, which will ensure the success of this venture. It is hereby approved that you can use our trademark of Pala at your place.

Thank you for your interest and cooperation.

Pala Hamburger

亲爱的李女士：

通过我公司的考察，我们深深地感到您与派乐之间存在着相呼应的理念，这将保证此事业的成功。我们特此准许您在您的店面使用我们的商标。

感谢您的兴趣与合作。

派乐汉堡

范例 6 | 出国进修申请

Dear Mr. Smith,

In order to improve my professional skill and offer better service for our company, I think I should learn more about current international sophisticated technology. I hereby advance an application for further study abroad.

I will ensure to study hard and come back to contribute more for our company's promising future! Your decision may influence our tomorrow. Please consider carefully.

Looking forward to your support!

Yours sincerely,

Tom

尊敬的史密斯先生：

为了提高职业技能，更好地服务于公司，我觉得我有必要学习更多的国际先进技术，所以我想向您申请出国深造的机会。

我保证会努力学习，并且回来后为我们公司的发展做出更大的贡献。您的决定可能会影响公司的未来，请您慎重考虑。

期望您的支持！

汤姆 谨上

邮件回复 *Reply*

Dear Tom,

I have discussed your case with other directors of the board. We have decided to approve your application for further study abroad. We will provide a fund to cover your training expense on the condition that you obtain the graduation certificate and are willing to work 3 more years for us.

We will arrange Mr. White of your section to take over your responsibility. Please ensure to complete the handover before you leave.

Yours sincerely,

John Smith

亲爱的汤姆：

我已与董事会的其他成员讨论过你的情况。我们决定同意你出国进修的申请，我们将会对你的培训费用予以报销，条件是你取得结业证书，并愿意再为公司服务3年。

你离开期间，我们安排你部门的怀特先生暂代你的职责。请在离开前确保做好交接工作。

约翰 · 史密斯 谨上

范例 7 | 调职申请

Dear Sir,

This is Tom Smith from Planning Section. I have worked here for more than 4 years since April 1, 2015. I have been doing my best to fulfill every task assigned to me, sparing no effort and pursuing perfection.

I have been devoting my energy and love to our company, and I really hope I could have long-term development here. Therefore, I want to know the company overall. As the Marketing Section is the leading department, which is in charge of our main business, I want to have a chance to enter this department to learn more. I promise I will work as hard in the new department as in my current department.

I desperately expect your permission.

Yours sincerely,

Tom Smith

尊敬的先生：

我是企划部的汤姆·史密斯，于2015年4月1日开始在这个部门工作，至今已经四年多的时间了。我一直很尽心尽力，严格要求自己，努力完成每项任务。

我对公司倾注了极大的精力和感情，我希望在这里得到长足发展，所以我想更全面地了解一下公司其他部门的工作。营销部是公司的重要部门，负责公司的主要业务。我希望可以得到机会，前往这个部门学习，我一定会像在现在这个部门一样努力工作。

热切盼望您的批准！

汤姆·史密斯 敬上

邮件回复 *Reply*

Dear Tom,

We received your application for a transfer, and had a discussion about it.

Complying with your request, we decide to transfer you to the Marketing Section.We arrange Zhang Ying, a new recruit to replace you. Please ensure to complete the handover before you leave.

Human Resource Section

亲爱的汤姆，

我们收到了你的调职申请，并就此进行了讨论。

应你的要求，我们将你调往营销部。你目前的职务由新聘人员张英接任，请务必做好交接工作。

人事部

范例 8 | 员工宿舍申请

Dear Sir,

This is Zhang Peng, a new staff member of the company. I live in Hanyang District, which is quite far away from our company, and it takes me almost 3 hours to commute everyday. In addition, the rents for apartments around the company are quite high, and it is difficult for me to afford renting a house. Therefore, I sincerely hope that the company can help me solve this major problem, so that I can work more energetically. I hereby apply for a dormitory.

Expecting your approval.

Truly yours,

Zhang Peng

尊敬的先生：

我是公司的新进员工张鹏。我来自汉阳区，我现在的居住地到单位路途较远，每天要花近3个小时在路上。另外，单位附近房屋普遍租金较高，在附近租房对我来说真的很困难。因此，我衷心地希望公司能够帮助我解决这个大难题，让我每天能够有充沛的精力更好地工作。特此向您申请宿舍一间。

恳望批准！

张鹏 敬上

邮件回复 *Reply*

Dear Mr. Zhang,

We have received your letter, asking for a dormitory. We are informing you that we have approved your application, since it is our duty to arrange accommodation for our staffs. We will allocate to you a furnished single room with a shower cubicle. You can move in once you go through the necessary procedures. Please come to our section for formalities in two days.

Logistics Group

亲爱的张先生：

我们收到了你关于申请宿舍的信。我们正式通知你我们已经核准了你的申请，为我们的员工安排住宿是我们的职责。我们给你分配的是一间带有淋浴间的单人房间。办理必要手续后你就可以入住。请在两天内到我部办理手续。

后勤部

范例 9 | 调换部门申请

Dear Mr. Zhang,

I am writing this letter in order to apply for working in a different department. Last month after we cooperated with the Marketing Department, I found I was interested in that department. I also learnt some marketing knowledge by myself. I think if I can be a member of the Marketing Department, I will have more enthusiasm and better work efficiency. On the other hand,the Marketing Department colleagues also recognize my ability. So I hope to be able to work for the Marketing Department.

I believe that interest is the best teacher. As long as I keep learning and accumulating work experience, I will do a better job. I hope you can consider my request. Thank you!

Best wishes!

Yours sincerely,

Tom

尊敬的张先生：

我写这封信的目的是为了申请换部门。自从上个月和市场营销部合作后，我发现自己对市场营销这个部门非常感兴趣，而且我也自学过市场营销的知识。我觉得自己到那个部门以后会有更大的工作热情和更高的工作效率。而且市场营销部的同事们非常认可我的能力。所以我希望能够调到市场营销部工作。

我相信兴趣是最好的老师，只要我不断学习，累积经验，我将会在这个部门工作得更出色。希望您能考虑我的请求。谢谢您！

祝好！

汤姆 谨上

邮件回复 *Reply*

Dear Tom,

I am very glad to receive your letter. We have considered your request and decided to approve your application. We think you are a quick learner and also innovative. I hope you can have a better performance there.

Best wishes!

Yours sincerely,

Zhang Ming

亲爱的汤姆：

很高兴收到你的来信。我们仔细考虑了你的要求，决定同意你调换部门的申请。我们认为你是一个学习能力很强，又具有创新力的员工。希望你调过去以后能够有更好的工作表现。

祝好！

张明 谨上

范例 10 | 购买新传真机申请

Dear Mr. Zhang,

Our fax machine of the finance department recently has broken, and the repair department also can't fix it. So we need a new one. We need this machine all the time to keep working. So I am writing to apply for a new fax machine as soon as possible. I am waiting for your approval.

Best wishes!

Yours sincerely,

Tom

尊敬的张先生：

我们财务部的传真机最近坏了，修理部门也没法修理，需要更换新的传真机。部门的工作一刻也离不开传真机。所以我们想要申请尽快购买一台新的传真机。希望您批准。

祝好！

汤姆 谨上

邮件回复 *Reply*

Dear Tom,

Your application has been approved. Fax machine will be sent to your office in the end of the month.

Best wishes!

Yours sincerely,

Zhang Ming

亲爱的汤姆：

你们的申请已经批准。传真机将会在这个月底送到你们的办公室。

祝好！

张明 谨上

范例 11 | 留学申请

Dear Mr. Zhang,

I am a senior student now and have learnt a lot during the four years. Our teachers help me a lot. Since my teacher mentioned the Washington University to me, I have been looking forward to studying in this school. So I want to apply to go to Washington University to study abroad.

Going to study in a foreign university is my dream, so I have always studied very hard, and ranked top in class. I also participated in many community activities to enrich my extra curricular life, and I exercised a lot from them. During the summer and winter vacations, I attended a variety of internships which had broadened my vision.

I'd like to go abroad and experience the different ways of teaching. So I expect to continue my study in Washington University. Please approve the application.

Best wishes!

Yours sincerely,

Tom

尊敬的张先生：

我现在是一名大四的学生，在这大学四年里学到了很多知识，老师们对我的帮助很大。在听老师讲到华盛顿大学的一些有关信息后，我非常向往。所以我想申请去华盛顿大学留学。

出国留学是我的梦想，所以一直以来我都很努力学习，成绩一直都在班里名列前茅。我还参加了很多社团活动，丰富我的课余生活，得到了很多的锻炼。在寒暑假我还参加多种实践活动，让我得以开阔视野。

我非常想去国外走走，感受一下国外的教育方式。所以，我希望去华盛顿大学留学进修。希望能够批准。

祝好！

汤姆 谨上

邮件回复 *Reply*

Dear Tom,

We know that you are an excellent student with strong abilities of both academic and practice. We agree that you are qualified to go abroad. So we approve your application.

Good luck!

Yours sincerely,

Zhang Ming

亲爱的汤姆：

我们知道你是个非常优秀的学生。具有很强的学术能力和实践能力。我们一致认为你非常符合申请出国留学的条件。我们同意你的申请。

祝好！

张明

读书笔记

Unit 5 通知篇

（1）如何写

书面通知一般包括5个部分：标题、称呼、正文、落款、日期。

a）标题一般写通知；称呼可以省略；

b）正文要简明扼要，写清楚通知的时间地点及事宜；

c）正文后面通常标有发通知的单位和日期。

（2）实用例句

a）Everyone is required to be present on time.

每个人都必须准时到场。

b）Notice is hereby given that...

现对……通知。

c）All teachers and students are required to attend the meeting on time.

全体师生务必准时参加会议。

d）The next Monthly Management Meeting, previously scheduled for Monday next week, has been rescheduled for Friday, May 11.

原定于下星期一的月度管理会议，已改为星期五，即5月11日。

e）According to the spirit of relevant documents.

根据相关文件的精神。

f）We are pleased to inform you that ...

我们很高兴通知您……

g）Please prepare your backup and helpdesk planning.

请做好后备的安排。

h）If overdue, may cause additional costs.

如果逾期，可能会产生额外费用。

i）We hope the new plans will lead to even better results.

我们期望新的计划会带来更好的结果。

范例 1 | 新任总经理上任通知

Dear Sirs,

This mail is to inform you that Mr. Smith has been appointed as your new manager responsible for your section. Mr. Smith obtained his master's degree of business administration from MIT and had rich experience in management. We believe you will get along with him very well since he is an amiable person.

As he is new to our company, you should try your best to assist his work. You can expect his appreciation if you can do your duties with chariness and responsibility as usual.

The Board
BBC Company

亲爱的先生们：

这封邮件是要通知你们史密斯先生已被任命为你们部门的新经理。史密斯先生获得了麻省理工学院的工商管理硕士学位，并且具有非常丰富的管理经验。同时，他也是一个非常和蔼的人，我们相信你们与他将相处得十分融洽。

由于他刚到我们公司，所以你们务必尽力协助他的工作。如果你们能一如既往地认真负责地履行职责，他将不胜感激。

BBC公司 董事会

邮件回复 *Reply*

Dear Sirs,

We are happy to hear that Mr. Smith will work with us from next week.

You can rest assured that we will do our utmost to assist his work, fulfilling the tasks he assigns and helping him adapt to the new environment as soon as possible. We believe his coming will enhance our teamwork and hence lead us to better achievements.

Yours faithfully,
All staffs of Marketing Department

尊敬的先生们：

我们很高兴得知从下周开始史密斯先生将和我们一起工作。

诸位请放心，我们一定会尽力协助他的工作，完成他交代的任务，帮助他尽快适应新的环境。我们相信他的到来会增强我们的团队协作力，带领我们取得更大的成绩。

销售部全体员工 敬上

范例 2 | 新员工到职通知

Dear Mr. Huang,

I am writing to inform you of the arrival of Mr. Zhang Hua, newly recruited by our company.

Mr. Zhang recently graduated from Nanjing University with a bachelor's degree in English literature. He passed our written examination and interview with good performance, proving himself a satisfactory candidate for the position of sales representative. We decided to give him the offer and arrange him to work in sales department.

He will arrive next Monday, March 30, please start his payroll from that day.

Enclosed please find the new recruit arrival notice.

Zhou Xiaofeng

Human Resources Section

亲爱的黄先生：

我写这封信是为了通知您我公司新进员工张华先生即将到职。

张先生刚从南京大学毕业，获英语文学学士学位。他以优异的成绩通过了我们的笔试和面试，证明自己是销售职位的合适人选。我们决定录用他，并安排他在销售部工作。

他到职的时间为下周一，即3月30日，请从该时间计算他的薪资。

附件请查收新入职人员的到岗通知。

人力资源部 周小峰

邮件回复 *Reply*

Dear Mr. Zhou,

We are writing to acknowledge receipt of your letter and the enclosed notice.

We welcome with pleasure the arrival of Mr. Zhang Hua and feel happy to work with a young man like him. We will try our best to help him with his work and his adaptation to the new environment.

Huang Yilong

Sales Department

亲爱的周先生：

我们收到了来信及附件中的通知。

我们欢迎张华先生的到来，并且很高兴能和这样一位年轻人一起工作。我们将尽力在工作上给他帮助，使他适应新的环境。

销售部 黄一龙

范例 3 | 辞职/卸任

Dear Sir or Madam:

Mr. Wang, the vice-president of our marketing, who has worked for over forty years, will be retiring at the end of March.

Michael, one of our top young managers, will be taking over Mr. Wang's responsibilities from March 20. Micheal will do his best to keep the good relationship that you and Mr. Wang have developed over the years.

Yours sincerely,

FOB Company

尊敬的先生/女士：

我公司营销副总裁王先生已为我公司服务40多年，将于三月底卸任。

我公司年轻高管之一迈克尔将于3月20日起接管王先生的职务。迈克尔将会尽全力维护您和王先生多年来建立的良好关系。

FOB公司 敬上

邮件回复 *Reply*

Dear Sir,

Thank your for your information about the retirement of Mr. Huang.

Mr. Huang is our old friend and has provided a lot of support when he is in office. It is a pity that we will not be able to cooperate with him in the future business. However, we also feel happy that he will be able to enjoy the leisure of his retired life and have more time to stay with his family.

We extend our congratulations to Michael for his promotion and we are quite willing to develop a good relation with him as we did with Mr. Wang.

Yours sincerely,

BBC Company

尊敬的先生：

感谢您通知我们黄先生卸任一事。

黄先生是我们的老朋友，在任期间为我们提供了很多帮助。很可惜以后在生意场合不能再与他一起合作了。但是，我们也为他感到高兴，因为他将尽情享受退休生活的闲暇，有更多的时间与家人共聚。

我们祝贺迈克尔晋升。我们也很愿意与他建立像王先生一样良好的关系。

BBC公司 敬上

范例 4 | 升职通知

Dear Michael,

Our vice-president, Mr. Wang will be retiring at the end of this month. We take pleasure to inform you that we have decided to appoint you as his replacement.

You have worked for our company for seven years and made great contributions to its development. We think it is the time for you to get a promotion. We believe you will lead our company to a more promising future.

The board

VVY Company

亲爱的迈克尔：

我们的副总裁王先生即将于本月底退休。我们很高兴地通知你我们决定将委派你为他的继任者。

你已经在我们公司工作了7年，为公司的发展做出过重大贡献。我们认为你应该得到晋升。我们相信你会给我们公司带来更加辉煌的未来。

VVY公司 董事会

邮件回复 *Reply*

Dear Sirs,

I am writing to extend my sincere gratitude to you for appointing me as the new vice-president. And I will work harder to live up to your trust.

Yours faithfully,

Michael

尊敬的先生们：

我写信是为了表达我诚挚的谢意，感谢你们任命我为公司副总裁。我会更加努力工作，不辜负诸位的信任。

迈克尔 敬上

范例 5 | 调职通知

Dear staff,

This is to notify the appointment of Mr. Tom Smith as the director of Advertising Department of ABC Company. Mr. Smith has 5-year's experience in advertising and we can expect his knowledge and experience will bring great value to our company.

Yours truthfully,

Augustine

尊敬的同事们：

本通知宣布汤姆·史密斯先生就任ABC公司广告部门总监一职。史密斯先生在广告推广方面拥有长达5年的工作经验，相信他的知识和阅历将会为本公司带来不可估量的价值。

奥古斯汀 谨上

邮件回复 *Reply*

Dear Augustine,

We're glad that Mr. Smith has been appointed as director of Advertising Department of ABC Company. We all have witnessed his performance in the past 5 years, and we will support him.

Yours,

All the staff

ABC Company

亲爱的奥古斯汀：

我们很高兴史密斯先生已经被任命为ABC公司广告部门主任。他在过去5年的表现我们有目共睹，我们完全支持他。

全体员工 谨上

ABC公司

范例 6 | 返职通知

Dear Mike,

I am writing to tell you that I have recovered from my recent appendicitis. I will come back to my post next Monday. I am looking forward to working with you again.

Many thanks for your comfort and support during my sickness.

Yours sincerely,

John

亲爱的麦克，

我写这封信是要告诉你我的盲肠炎已经痊愈。下周一我将返职。我期待再次与你一起工作，并且希望不久能收到你的来信。

感谢你在我生病期间给予我的安慰和支持。

约翰 敬上

邮件回复 *Reply*

Dear John,

I am happy to hear that you have recovered and you will come back. You can't imagine how much we miss you. We are all expecting to meet you in great form.

Yours sincerely,

Mike

亲爱的约翰：

我很高兴你已经恢复，并且即将返职。你简直不能想象我们多么想念你。我们都期待见到一个精神焕发的你。

麦克 敬上

范例 7 | 公司开业通知

Dear Sir or Madam,

We are so honored to remind you that because of the rapid increase in our trade, we've decided to set another branch for our products here in Caidian on April 1.We've employed a number of counselors as well as a professional service group, which makes routine checks on all equipment bought from us.

We will be extremely pleased if you take full advantage of our services and comfortable shopping environment as well.We are sure to gurantee the quality of our products.

Genuinely yours,

Peter

尊敬的先生 / 女士：

我们很荣幸地通知您，因为业务量激增，我们决定将于4月1号在蔡甸开设另一家分公司来销售我们的产品。我们聘请了一组咨询顾问和一支专业的服务团队，负责日常检查从我公司购买的设备。

本公司很高兴您能充分利用我们的服务和舒适的购物环境，本公司保证产品的质量。

彼得 敬上

邮件回复 *Reply*

Dear Peter,

We've just received your notice telling that you will set a new branch. Congratulations on it! We are so glad from the bottom of our hearts as you have always been putting our interests first.

We will always support your services and enjoy your shopping environment all the time. Wish you a good business and more benefits. Congratulations once again on your going to open up a new branch!

Best wishes!

Tony

亲爱的彼得：

我们刚收到了您的通知告知您将开设一家新的分公司，祝贺您！我们发自心底的高兴因为您一直把我们的利益摆在首位。

我们将始终支持您的服务并享受您提供的购物环境。祝您生意兴隆，财源广进。再一次祝贺您即将开设新的分公司！

致以我们良好的祝愿！

托尼

范例 8 | 暂停营业通知

Dear Peter,

I am writing to inform you that our supermarket in Caidian District will be temporarily closed right from March 25 to March 31, resulting from renovations to the interior layout.

We are to open up once again on April 1, and we ensure to inform you of any update information then.

We are genuinely sorry for the inconvenience we have brought to you.

Best regards,

Chris

尊敬的彼得：

我写信是要通知您，因为我们在蔡甸区的超市将要再次装潢翻新，由此，我们打算在3月25日到3月31日暂停营业一星期。

我们将定在4月1号重新开张。一旦其间有任何消息，我们确保会通知您。

我们真诚地为此次暂停营业给您造成的不便表示歉意。

致以我们良好的祝愿！

克里斯

邮件回复 *Reply*

Dear Chris,

I am writing to thank you for your informing us of the news.

You've always been attaching great importance to the quality of your products and service, which I really appreciate. You have done a good job and I believe, after the renovations, everything will go much better than before. Wish you to achieve rapid progress and great success in running your own business.

Yours,

Peter

亲爱的克里斯：

我感谢您告知这一消息。

您一直以来都非常重视您的产品和服务，对此我很感激。您做得很好并且我认为您在装潢翻新之后一切都会变得比以前更好。祝您在经营您的生意中取得快速进展和巨大成功。

彼得 谨上

范例 9 | 营业时间变更通知

Dear clients,

We are honored to notify the following:

Right from April 1, 2019,on our new shop hours would be changed to — from 9 in the morning to 9 in the evening, Monday to Friday.

We genuinely wish that the time shift will enable us to offer you the most effective and considerate services.

Genuinely yours,

Zhongbai Corporation

尊敬的客户：

我们非常荣幸地在这做出以下宣布：

从2019年4月1号起，我们的工作时间将改为周一至周五的早上九点至晚上九点。

我们真心希望我们工作时间的及时变动能让我们为你们提供最有效同时也是最贴心的服务。

中百公司 谨上

邮件回复 *Reply*

Dear Manger,

I'm writing to thank you for informing us your time change and I think we would have no trouble in adapting to it.

I'd also like to thank you for your always providing us with the most effective and considerate services.

Wish you progress and success sincerely!

Yours,

Peter

尊敬的总经理先生：

我感谢贵公司通知我们你们的时间变动，我想我们适应起来应该没有任何问题。

同时我也感谢您一直以来提供给我们最有效同时也是最贴心的服务。

真诚地祝您取得更大进步并获得成功！

彼得 谨上

范例 10 | 公司搬迁/电话号码变更通知

Dear Sirs,

At our company meeting on March 25, it was decided to move our company from the current address to No.3000 Dongfeng Road. In the meanwhile, there was also a crucial change on our telephone number, please always feel free to contact us at 027–88888888 anytime within our office hours!

We will appreciate it if you inform the related departments of the above changes.

Yours faithfully,

John

敬启者:

在公司3月25号的会议上，我们公司的地址已决定改为东风大道3000号，同时公司的联系电话也由原号码变更为现在的027–88888888，欢迎各位在办公时间内随时与我们联系。

如您能把这些变化通知相关部门，我们将不胜感激。

约翰 谨上

邮件回复 *Reply*

Dear Manager,

I'm writing to thank you for your notice of your company's new site, and we have also kept a record of your new telephone number.

We will undoubtedly deliver the changes to the related departments.

Faithfully yours,

Edward

尊敬的总经理先生:

我写信给您感谢您确认您公司的新地址，我们已记录下了您的新电话号码。

我们当然会把这些变化通知相关部门。

爱德华 谨上

范例 11 | 公司停业通知

Dear × × ×,

With the demolition of our premises at the above address under a development scheme, the part of our business carried on there will be discontinued after the end of March.

On Sunday, March 27, we are hosting a closing-out sale. Stock on hand will be cleared in spite of down as much as one half.

Stock to be cleared is unrivaled in both variety and quality. As is possible to be very well attended, we wish you would like to visit our store during the opening days as early as possible.

Yours sincerely,

× × ×

尊敬的× × ×，

在经营重组计划下，上述经营场所要被取消，该处的业务将于3月底后停止。

在3月27号（星期日），我们将组织一次清仓销售。现有存货的折价达一半之多。

清仓商品无论种类还是数量都无可挑剔。因此次销售参加人员可能很多，我们希望您在清仓销售期间尽早来。

× × × 谨上

邮件回复 *Reply*

Dear × × ×,

I'm writing to thank you for your notice that the part of your business carried on there will be discounted after the end of March and you are hosting a closing-out sale.

Thank you for your information and we are sure to visit your store as early as we can to support your business.

Yours,

× × ×

尊敬的× × ×：

写这封电子邮件是为了感谢您的通知，您该处的业务将与3月底停止，并且您将组织一次清仓销售。

感谢您的提醒，而且我们确保会在您清仓销售期间尽早来支持您的生意。

× × × 谨上

范例 12 | 缴费通知

Dear Resident,

This is for notifying you that you have to pay a gas bill of ￥100 of March.

You have consumed 25 m^3 gas this month, and we set each CBM at 4 yuan, which adds up to the total amount of 100 yuan.

To make it more convenient for you to pay the gas bills and improve our work efficiency, we genuinely advise you to pay the gas bill by bank transfer.

I thank you a lot on behalf of our corporation for your understanding and support all along!

Yours,

Gas Company

尊敬的住户：

此函通知您需缴纳3月份燃气费100元。

本月您共使用天然气25m^3，每立方米单价4元，所以总计金额为100元。

为了方便缴纳燃气费并提高工作效率，我们诚挚建议用户通过银行转账方式缴纳燃气费。

我谨代表本公司非常感谢您一直以来给予的理解和支持！

天然气公司 谨上

邮件回复 *Reply*

Dear Manager,

I have received your bill and after I check the records, I find no error of the statistic.

Enclosed is a check to cover my bill, please check the amount and send me a confirmation a bit later.

Thanks!

Yours,

Edward

尊敬的总经理先生：

我已收到你的账单，经我核实，一切数据均没有错。

随信附上一张支票支付账单，请核对数日，并稍后寄送一张确认书给我。

谢谢！

爱德华 谨上

范例 13 | 公司盘点通知

Dear distinguished consumers and suppliers,

Thanks a million for your kind support and cooperation all the way!

I'm writing to remind you that our annual stocktaking is to be from March 27 to 31, 2020. There will be a temporary stop on all of our delivering and receiving operations. Accordingly, it has been decided that there would be no goods delivery to all of our warehouses except special requests delivered by your Purchasing Department. We are going to resume the normal delivering and receiving operations from April 1.

We sincerely make apologies for any inconvenience caused by us.

Genuinely yours

Wuhan Logistics Co.

尊敬的客户及供应商：

非常感谢各位一直以来的支持与合作！

特此通知本公司将于2020年3月27至31日进行盘点，盘点期间，所有送货、收货业务将会暂停。如遇特殊情况，请各单位采购部告知，本公司会做出相应安排。本公司将于2020年4月1号起正式恢复运营。

本公司真诚地为给各位带来的任何不便表示歉意！

武汉物流公司 谨上

邮件回复 *Reply*

Dear Manager,

I'm hearing from you that you are now under your annual stocktaking thus stopping on all of our delivering and receiving operations. I can fully understand it. I will contact your Purchasing Department in case we meet with specific circumstances.

Wish your company will resume the normal delivering and receiving operations as early as possible.

Yours,

× × ×

尊敬的总经理先生：

我刚得知您在进行盘点，所以所有送货、收货业务将会暂停。我表示理解，如遇特殊情况，我将联系贵公司采购部。

希望贵公司能尽快正式恢复经营。

× × × 谨上

范例 14 | 求职录用通知

Dear × × ×,

You have been selected as a secretary to Mr. Li, director of the Marketing Department. We would like you to report for work on April 1.

Please arrive at 8:00 a.m. on April 1, and get Miss Liu in Personnel, where you will spend an hour or so filling out the necessary forms and learning the company's employment policies. Then Miss Liu will introduce you to all staff in the Marketing Department.

VOA Company

亲爱的 × × ×：

我们决定聘您为本公司营销部经理李先生的秘书。希望您于4月1日来公司报到上班。

请您于4月1日早晨8点到人事处找刘小姐。您将花一小时左右的时间填写一些必要的表格并学习公司的就业法规，然后刘小姐会把您介绍到营销部。

VOA公司 谨上

邮件回复 *Reply*

Dear Manager,

I'm so delighted to have heard from you that I'd been employed as a secretary in your company. Thank you for giving me the precious chance. I will report for work as you required.

I'm looking forward to working with you.

Yours faithfully,

Edward

亲爱的经理：

我很高兴听到你的消息，我被聘任为您公司的一名秘书，谢谢您给我宝贵的机会。我会按照要求到公司报到。

我期待着与你们共事。

爱德华 谨上

读书笔记

范例 15 | 公司裁员通知

Dear Peter,

We had been trying our every effort to keep all of our employs during this hard period of reorganization. Unfortunately, this is not the case.

It is with deep regret that I must inform you of the recent decision to terminate your association with our company. Recent financial problems have forced us to scrutinize our manpower resources carefully and therefore, several employees have been unfortunately dismissed in the process. Wish you a rather promising future!

Yours faithfully ,

ABC Company

亲爱的彼得：

在公司重组的困难时期，我们一直努力设法保留公司的全体员工，但遗憾的是这个愿望很难实现。

非常抱歉我必须通知您最近决定终止您与我公司的合作。近来经济问题使我们仔细审查了我们的人力资源部门，因此，有些雇员将在这个过程中要被不幸裁掉。

祝福您有一个锦绣前程!

ABC公司 谨上

邮件回复 *Reply*

Dear Manager,

I'm sorry that our company is under this hard situation, it is a tough time for you to go through. I can fully understand it. However, I feel it quite unfair to be dismissed since I have worked for you for more than ten years and it is hard to get a new job elsewhere at my age. I hope you can take my stand point and reconsider your decision.

I am looking forward to your early reply.

Yours faithfully,

Peter

亲爱的经理：

我们公司处在这样的艰难时期，对你们来说也很困难,我能理解你们的决定。但是，我还是觉得不公平，我为公司服务已经有10多年的时间，以我现在的年纪在别处很难找到工作。我希望您能站在我的立场上重新考虑一下您的决定。

期待您早日回复。

彼得 谨上

范例 16 | 节假日通知

Dear staff,

To express our gratitude for your excellent work this month and enable everyone to spend the Mid-autumn Festival with your family, we've decided to close the office from August 31 to September 3(inclusive). All personnel will be given paid leave during this period.

Wish you a happy holiday.

× × ×

致全体员工：

为了表示对各位这个月来辛勤工作的感谢，同时也为了各位能和家人一起尽情享受中秋节，我们决定从8月31号当天放假直至9月3日（包括3日在内）。这段时间里，所有员工都将享受带薪休假。

希望大家有一个快乐的假期。

× × × 谨上

邮件回复 *Reply*

Dear Manager,

We are happy that our work this month has been appreciated and that we will be given paid leave during the Mid-autumn Festival.Thank you for your generosity, and for your really caring for us all, we promise to work harder right after the holiday.

Yours,

All staff

亲爱的经理：

我们很高兴这个月的工作已经被人们重视，这样，我们在中秋节将可以带薪休假。我们对您的慷慨表示谢意,感谢你真心地关心我们所有人,我们承诺假期后一定会更努力地工作。

全体员工 谨上

范例 17 | 商品出货通知

Dear Mr. Frank,

We hereby notify that we have shipped your order No.2019 of March 1, 2019. And please check the relevant shipping documents I have faxed to you.

If everything is OK, you will receive the goods you ordered by April 1, 2019.

Please inform us of your receipt of the consignments as soon as they arrive. Thanks in advance for your cooperation!

Yours genuinely,

DIY Corporation

尊敬的弗兰克先生：

我们通知您，您2019年3月1日所下的2019号订单的货物已发出。关于发货的信息已经通过传真发送给您，请您查收。

如果不出任何意外的话，您最迟将在2019年4月1号收到货物。

货一到请您在第一时间通知我们。提前感谢您的合作！

DIY公司 谨上

邮件回复 *Reply*

Dear × × ×,

Thank you for having shipped our order No.2019 of March 1, 2019. I will check the relevant shipping documents you have sent to me and I will keep checking the goods, as I've been looking forward to them. I promise I'll inform you the instant they arrive.

Thank you for your cooperation too.

Yours,

Frank

亲爱的× × ×：

感谢您为我方2019年3月1日所下的2019号订单发货。我会查看相关的装运单据，并检验这些货物，我一直期待着它们的到来。我保证货物一抵达就会通知你方。

同样感谢你方合作。

弗兰克 谨上

范例 18 | 商品订购通知

Dear distinguished members,

We are happy to inform you that you could order any commodities that you want as before. What you need to do is to firstly log on our website and then choose what you are into on it, and take down your detailed address. And we will arrange the delivery upon the time we receive your order.

Wish you will enjoy our service all the time!

Yours truly,

Pacific Department Store

尊敬的会员朋友：

很高兴通知大家，每位顾客朋友现在都可以像以前一样正常订购商品了。您只要先登录我们的官网并在网页上选择好您需要的本店商品，然后留下您的详细地址。收到您的订单，我们就会安排送货服务。

希望您能喜欢我们的服务！

大洋百货 谨上

邮件回复 *Reply*

Dear Manager,

We are glad to hear that we could order commodities on line as before. Thank you for your information. And we will support you as usual.

Yours,

× × ×

亲爱的经理：

我们也很高兴得知我们可以像以前一样网上订购商品了。感谢您的通知。我们会一如既往地支持你们。

× × × 谨上

读书笔记

范例 19 | 商品缺货通知

Dear subscribers,

Because of expanding sales, we feel very sorry for having to inform you that *Alice in Wonderland* has all been sold out.

However, we are replenishing our stock. Please contact us to confirm whether you'd like it to be delivered by mail or express if you still want to place an order with us.

I'm always looking forward to your reply at your earliest convenience.

Yours,

Taobao

尊敬的订购客户：

因为销售量剧增，我们很抱歉地通知您，您订购的《爱丽丝漫游奇境记》已经脱销了。

不过我们正在抓紧进货。如果您还想要订购，那么请告知我们发货方式，是平邮还是快递？

期待您尽快回复。

淘宝网 谨上

邮件回复 *Reply*

Dear ×××,

I feel sorry to hear that *Alice in Wonderland* has all been sold out, since it has always been one of my favorite works. I still want to place an order with you. Would you mind informing me the moment your new stock has come? Thank you in advance!

I'm looking forward to your earliest reply.

Yours,

Leo

亲爱的×××：

我很遗憾地听说《爱丽丝漫游奇境记》已经售完，这本书一直是我最喜欢的作品之一。我依然愿意从你处订购。请您在有了新的存货时通知我，好吗？提前向您表示感谢。

期待您的早日回复。

利奥 谨上

范例 20 | 付款确认通知

Dear Joyce,

On March 25, 2019, the amount of ￥100,000,000 as payment for your invoice No.1234567 was transferred into your account. Please check and send us your confirmation.

I have faxed a copy of the remittance slip for your reference.

Truly yours,

Edward

尊敬的乔伊斯：

2019年3月25日，我方已经将发票号码为1234567的货款100000000元人民币汇入您的账户里。请您查收并确认。

汇款凭单我也已经传真给您，以供参考。

爱德华 谨上

邮件回复 *Reply*

Dear Edward,

I have received your mail informing that the amount of ￥ 100,000,000 as payment for my invoice No.1234567 has been transferred into my account. Thank you for your cooperation.

Yours,

Joyce

亲爱的爱德华：

我收到您的邮件，告知你方已经将发票号码为1234567的货款100000000元人民币汇入我的账户。非常感谢您的合作。

乔伊斯 谨上

读书笔记

范例 21 | 样品寄送通知

Dear Mr. Benjemin,

I'm now writing to inform you that the samples that you requested were sent by Federal Express today.

In the mail, I've also enclosed a price list and color swatches. Please inform me at your earliest convenience as soon as they arrive. Thanks a lot!

I'm looking forward to your earliest response.

Yours sincerely,

BBC Company

尊敬的本杰明先生：

我写这封信是要通知您，您要求的样品已于今天由联邦快递发出。

随信附上了价格表和颜色样本。您收到货物时请通知我。非常感谢！

期待您的尽快回应。

BBC公司 谨上

邮件回复 *Reply*

Dear Sirs,

I'm happy to be informed that the samples that we requested are on the way. We will confirm the receipt of them as soon as they arrive. Thank you for your cooperation.

Yours,

Benjemin

亲爱的先生：

我很高兴得知样品已经寄出。我们收到后就会向你方确认。感谢合作。

本杰明 谨上

范例 22 | 入账金额不足通知

Dear Mr. Jeff,

We've already received the telegraphic transfer of ¥ 10,000 on March 25, 2019. However, I am afraid that you have neglected something, that's the cost of freight and insurance that was indicated on the invoice we faxed to you.

We would therefore like to ask you to transfer an additional ¥800 so that we can arrange the shipment the soonest possible.

We are going to deliver you the goods immediately after we receive the full payment.

Best regards!

Midea Corporation

尊敬的杰夫先生：

2019年3月25日，您电汇的10000元人民币到账了，但是恐怕您忘记加上运输和保险费用了。那些费用我们曾经在传真给您的发票上标明了。

为此我们想请您补足800元，这样我们就可以安排装船。

只要收到全额货款，我们就会立即发货。

致以良好的祝愿！

美的集团

邮件回复 *Reply*

Dear Sirs,

I'm sorry to admit that I just forgot the cost of freight and insurance, as I've been so busy these days. I will transfer an additional RMB 800 right away. Please check.

Yours,

Jeff

亲爱的先生：

我很抱歉地承认,这些天我太忙以致忘了运费和保险费。我将支付额外的800元，请查收。

杰夫 谨上

范例 23 | 取消活动通知

Notice

The sports meeting previously scheduled for tomorrow has been canceled because of the heavy rain. Each grade has classes according to the schedule as normal. The specific time of holding the sports meeting will be advised later. All group leaders of each grade should arrange the related work well to ensure the normal teaching activities.

President Office

September 21th, 2019

通知

由于大雨，原定于明天的运动会取消。各年级按课表正常上课。举行运动会的具体时间将另行通知。各年级负责人做好相关工作以确保正常教学活动。

校长室

2019年9月21日

读书笔记

Unit 6 感谢篇

（1）如何写

a）首先表达对对方的庆贺、慰问、款待和帮忙的感谢；

b）表达自己的感想，赞扬对方，语气要真诚；

c）送上祝福和感谢。

（2）实用例句

a）Thank you for your concern about my baby.

谢谢你对我孩子的关心。

b）It is kind of you to send me a birthday present.

谢谢你送我这个生日礼物。

c）I really appreciate your wishes.

我真的很感谢你的祝福。

d）It is good to hear from you to give me such an important advice.

能够收到你的来信我很高兴，谢谢你给我的这个重要的建议。

e）Please accept my thanks not only for the letter but also for the good wishes.

请接受我的谢意，不仅是因为你的来信，也为你的祝福。

f）I am so happy to have a friend like you who always give me so much help and support.

我很高兴能有你这样的朋友，经常给我很多帮助和支持。

g）Your letter gives me so much comfort and happiness and reminds me that I have such a good friend.

你的来信给了我很大的安慰和快乐，提醒了我有这样一个知心的朋友在我的身边。

h）Thank you once again.

再次表示感谢。

i）Give my best wishes to you!

祝你一切都好！

范例 1 | 感谢邀请

Dear Mr. Lin,

Thank you for your invitation. I shall be very delighted to attend your opening ceremony on Monday morning, May 16th. I know it is your long-cherished wish to have a company of your own and you have finally made it come true. This is due to your outstanding wisdom, your superior judgment and great efforts for so long a time. I felt so happy when I heard the news. Congratulations! And of course, I will be there on this exciting moment.

I will arrive at your company at about 8:00 a.m. that day and send my congratulations and best wishes in person. I am looking forward to witnessing the establishment of your company and your new career.

Congratulations again!

Yours sincerely,

Linda

亲爱的林先生：

感谢您的邀请。我非常高兴出席贵公司于5月16日，星期一早上举行的开业典礼。我知道您一直以来的心愿就是拥有一家自己的公司，现在您的梦想终于成真了。这一切都是您非凡的智慧、过人的胆识和长期努力的结果。听到这一消息，我感到由衷的高兴。恭喜您！在这一激动人心的时刻，我当然会出现在那里。

我会于当天上午8点左右到达贵公司，亲自恭贺并送上我美好的祝愿。我期待着见证您公司的诞生以及您的新事业的起步。

再次恭喜您！

琳达 谨上

读书笔记

邮件回复 Reply

Dear Linda,

I received your letter on Mar. 25 and I am happy that you can be here to accompany us at our opening ceremony. It will be a great honor to have your presence on the event.

We have arranged a feast after the ceremony and you will have the opportunity to taste genuine Hubei food. A visit to our new company will be followed after the feast before your trip back to Shanghai. And my secretary will drive you to the airport. By the way, we will pay the air tickets for your round trip. I hope you will like our arrangements.

Yours sincerely,

Lin Feng

亲爱的琳达：

我收到了您3月25日的来信。您能出席我们的开业典礼，我感到非常高兴。您的光临是我们莫大的荣幸。

我们在典礼后安排了宴会，您将有机会品尝到地道的湖北菜肴。宴会之后，在您回上海之前，我们安排您参观我们的新公司。然后，我的秘书会送您去机场。另外，您往返的机票我们全部负责。希望您喜欢我们这样的安排。

真诚的林峰

读书笔记

范例 2 | 感谢款待

Dear Mr. Lin,

I am writing to thank you for your hospitality when I visited Wuhan last Monday when I attended your opening ceremony. It was really a big event. I was very happy to see the smiles on your face when you cut the red ribbon.

The visit to your new company impressed me a lot. Watching those sections and devices, I knew you were ushering another success in your life.

Best wishes to you and your company!

Yours sincerely,

Linda

亲爱的林先生：

上周一我去武汉参加您公司的开业典礼，受到了您热情的款待，特致信表达我的谢意。那天的场面热闹非凡。看到您剪彩时脸上洋溢的笑意，我感到非常高兴。

参观您的新公司给我留下了深刻的印象。看到那些部门和设施，我知道您正迎来人生更大的辉煌。

祝福您和您的公司！

琳达 谨上

邮件回复 *Reply*

Dear Linda,

I am happy to hear that you enjoyed your trip to Wuhan last Monday and was satisfied with our arrangements for you. I hope you can make another trip to here in the future and I can entertain you better.

I have sent you ten cans of lotus root and pork soup that I bought from a local supermarket. They may not taste so good as the dish you had in the restaurant that day, but I hope you will like it. Notice the coming of the parcel.

Yours sincerely,

Lin Feng

亲爱的琳达：

很高兴听你说对上周的武汉之行及我们为你做的安排感到满意。我希望以后你还会到这里来，让我好好招待你一番。

我给你寄去了十罐莲藕排骨汤，是从当地的超市购买的。味道可能没有那天在餐馆里吃的那么好，希望你能喜欢。请注意查收包裹！

林峰 谨上

范例 3 | 感谢参访

Dear Prof. Smith,

How are you recently? Your last visit to our company provided a good opportunity for us to learn from an expert in computer science. Your speech rich in wisdom and vision was really impressive. Your suggestions about the development of software industry are constructive and we believe they will be helpful for the development of our company too. We express our heart-felt gratitude to you for your coming, sharing your time, knowledge and energy with us. And we are expecting another opportunity to entertain you better. You will be always welcomed here.

Best wishes for you and your family!

Yours sincerely,

Lin Feng

尊敬的史密斯教授：

最近好吗？您上次到公司的参访为我们提供了一个良好的机会，可以向计算机科学领域的专家请教学习。您的讲演充满智慧和远见，给我们留下了深刻的印象。您就软件行业发展提出了建设性的意见，相信对我们公司的发展也是大有裨益的。我们对您的到访表示由衷的谢意，感谢您抽时间和我们分享您丰富的知识和充沛的活力。我们期待着还有机会能让我们更好地尽地主之谊。随时欢迎您再访。

祝福您和您的家人！

林峰 敬上

读书笔记

邮件回复 *Reply*

Dear Mr. Lin,

I have received your letter of May 16th, and thank you for your compliments. I am really flattered that you spoke so highly of me and my visit to your company. I am very happy to be of some help to you.

I enjoyed my trip very much and was impressed by your hospitality. And I want to thank you for your utmost cordiality. I am also looking forward to meeting you another time.

Yours sincerely,

White Smith

亲爱的林先生：

我收到了您5月16日的来信，感谢您对我的溢美之词。您对我本人及我的贵公司之行给予那么高的评价实在令我受宠若惊。我很高兴能对你们有所帮助。

上次的行程我很满意，你们的热情好客给我留下了深刻的印象。感谢你们盛情的款待。期待有机会与你们再次会面。

怀特·史密斯 谨上

读书笔记

范例 4 | 感谢建议

Dear Madam,

Thank you for your letter in which you provided an excellent idea on the improvement of our products. We have studied the problem you described and concluded that this defect did cause inconvenience to our customers. We have to say "thank you" for telling us this problem so that we can have a chance to overcome it and make our products more customer-friendly. We will take your proposal into consideration when we design next generation of the product.

To express our heart-felt gratitude, we send you a sample of one of our new products as a gift.

Yours sincerely,
ABC Company
By John Brown

亲爱的夫人：

感谢您的来信，您在信中为我们的产品改进提出了一个非常好的建议。我们已经就您提出的问题进行了研究，发现我们的产品存在的这一缺点确实会给我们的顾客带来不便。感谢您为我们提出这一问题，让我们有机会克服缺点，使我们的产品更加符合客户的要求。我们在设计下一代产品的时候一定会将您的建议考虑进去。

为了表达我们由衷的感谢，我们给您寄去了一份新产品的样品作为礼物。

ABC公司
约翰 · 布朗 敬上

读书笔记

邮件回复 *Reply*

Dear Mr. Brown,

Thank you for your gift. It is quite practical and I like it very much. I had planned to buy one, and you sent it to me. A wonderful coincidence, right?

I am just an ordinary customer, and I think I have the responsibility to make my life more comfortable and convenient. In this sense, I wrote the letter not only for you but also for me and many others like me. And I am happy you can accept my points.

Yours faithfully,

Jane Jones

亲爱的布朗先生：

谢谢您的礼物。这份礼物非常实用，我很喜欢。我原本想买一台，您正好给我送了一个，真是巧，不是吗？

我只是普通顾客中的一名，我想我有责任使自己的生活更加舒适便利。从这个意义上讲，我写那封信不仅是为了你们，也是为了我自己和那些同我一样的其他顾客。我很高兴你们能够接受我的建议。

忠实的顾客

简·琼斯 谨上

读书笔记

范例 5 | 感谢关照

Dear Jane,

I can't tell you how greatly I appreciate all you have done for me these days and how grateful I am for the comfort and encouragement you gave me when I needed them so desperately.

No one knows better than you that what a great loss that business failure brought to my company and what a big hit it meant to me. But I am trying to take your advice and I will work harder for the future of my company and my employees.

I really do not know what I would have been without you. Thank you again for everything you have done for me!

Yours sincerely,

Lin Feng

亲爱的简：

这些天你为我做的一切，我的谢意无法言表。在我最需要安慰和鼓励的时候，你无私地给予了我，我深表感激。

没有人比你更了解，这次生意失败对我的公司来说是一个多么大的损失，而对于我而言是一个多么沉重的打击。但是我正在尝试着采纳你的建议，我会更加努力地工作，为了我公司的未来，也为了我的雇员的前途。

真不知道如果没有你情况会怎么样。再次感谢你为我所做的一切！

林峰 谨上

邮件回复 *Reply*

Dear Lin,

I am delighted to hear that you are trying to step out of the shadow of that failure. I believe you can revive your company with your wisdom, your persistence, and especially your love for your employees.

If you need my help, please don't hesitate to let me know!

Yours sincerely,

Jane

亲爱的林：

很高兴听到你说你正试着走出上次生意失败的阴影。我相信凭着你的智慧、坚韧，尤其是你对员工们的责任心，你一定会使你的公司重新振作起来。

如果你需要我的帮助，请随时告知我！

简 谨上

范例 6 | 感谢合作

Dear Mr. Smith,

I am very glad to see that our last deal has settled, and happy to hear that you are satisfied with the products we provided. I have to say this is a mutually beneficial exchange. Personally, I appreciate your decisiveness and humor, which impressed me so much. We are looking forward to another chance to cooperate with you.

Thank you again for your interest and cooperation in maintaining a good exchange partnership.

With thanks and regards!

Yours truly,

Lin Feng

亲爱的史密斯先生：

很高兴看到我们上一次的交易成功进行，听说你们对于我们产品很满意，我很欣慰。不得不说这是一次互惠的生意。我个人对您的果断和幽默非常欣赏，印象十分深刻。我们期待着还有机会能与你们合作。

再次感谢你们维持良好贸易伙伴关系的兴趣和合作。

献上诚挚的感谢和祝福！

林峰 敬上

邮件回复 *Reply*

Dear Mr. Lin,

I received your letter of May 18. I agree with you that the deal was a mutually beneficial one. We have gained great profits through the cooperation with Chinese exporters in recent years, and we are keenly desirous of expending our trade with you in home appliance. We really hope we could have further cooperation with each other and achieve greater development together.

With best regards!

Yours sincerely,

John Smith

亲爱的林先生：

我收到了您5月18日的来信。您认为我们上次的生意是互惠的，这点我十分赞同。近年来，我们通过与中国的出口商合作获利颇丰，我们迫切期望扩大与你们在家电行业的贸易合作。我们真心希望能继续与您深入合作，将来获得巨大发展。

献上最诚挚的祝福！

约翰 · 史密斯 敬上

范例 7 | 感谢咨询

Dear Mrs. Brown,

Thank you for your consultation regarding the lady shaver CD 2215. This is a new model developed by our company and it was launched last month. We are now planning to promote it in a large scale. The detailed information has been sent to you today. Please kindly check. If you have further doubts about this product, please contact Miss Li at our Service Department. Her direct number is 86-021-78912325.

Thanks again for your attention and support.

Yours sincerely,
Lily Chen
ABC Company

亲爱的布朗夫人：

非常感谢您来信垂询我公司生产的CD 2215 型号的女性剃毛器。这是我们新开发的一种型号，已于上月发布。目前，我们正在策划针对这一产品的大型促销活动。详细的信息数据已经于今天寄送给您，请您注意查收。如果您对我公司的这项产品还有其他疑问，请直接联系客服部的李小姐，她的电话是86-021-78912325。

再次感谢您的关注和支持。

ABC公司
陈莉莉 敬上

读书笔记

邮件回复 *Reply*

Dear Ms. Chen,

Thank you for your letter dated March 18 and the enclosed material. I was deeply impressed by the products' unique design and was convinced that it would meet customers' demand in our market. In addition, I believe a company establishing such a well-known brand is worth trusting that it will provide products of high quality and satisfactory service. Could you please send me a specific price catalogue? If the price you provide is attractive, I will consider placing an order with you.

Yours sincerely,

Lucy Brown

尊敬的陈女士：

你方3月18日的来函收悉，感谢寄送的材料。该产品的设计独特，我相信会迎合本地市场消费者的需求。另外，我相信贵公司创办了如此知名的品牌，一定是值得信赖的，提供的产品质量应该是上乘的，服务也应当是令人满意的。你们能否寄送一份详尽的价格目录给我？如果你们提供的价格有吸引力，那么我会考虑下订单。

露西 · 布朗 谨上

读书笔记

范例 8 | 感谢订购

Dear Sirs,

We acknowledge with thanks receipt of your letter dated March 22, and the enclosed order. Their full contents have obtained our immediate attention. We have carefully noted all the specifications shown on your order and are happy to see that our cooperation has been further promoted.

We are enclosing herewith our sales confirmation in duplicate. Please kindly sign and return a copy with your duly signature. In addition, we would like to remind you to open a letter of credit in our favor in time so that we can arrange production and shipment as soon as possible.

We will do our best to maintain the good quality of our products, and will make the best effort to meet your special requirements. We sincerely hope that you will place further orders with us very soon if the execution of this order proves satisfaction to you.

Yours sincerely,

ABC Company

尊敬的先生：

感谢贵方3月22日的来信及附上的订单。我方马上就关注了信上及订单的内容。我方已经仔细地注意了贵方订单中列举的所有事项，并且高兴地发现我们的合作已经更进了一步。

我方随函附上我方的销售确认书两份。请贵方签名且寄还及时签名的一张复本给我方。另外，我方想提醒贵方及时开具以我方为受益人的信用证以便我们尽快安排生产及装船事项。

我方将尽全力来维持我方货物的品质，尽全力来达到贵方的特别要求。我方诚意地希望，如果这次订单的执行结果令贵方满意，不久贵方会下进一步的订单给我方。

ABC公司 敬上

读书笔记

邮件回复 *Reply*

Dear Sirs,

We acknowledge receipt of your letter of March 24, and the enclosed sales confirmation. We thank you for your prompt attention.

In compliance with your instruction, we are sending you a copy of confirmation with our signature. And we have opened a letter of credit through China Bank, which is in strict compliance with the terms and shipment as specified. For the two documents, please check the enclosure.

We hope this cooperation will further develop our mutually beneficial partnership.

Yours sincerely,

DEL Company

尊敬的先生：

贵方3月24日来函及销售确认书附件收悉。我方对你方的立刻关照表示感谢。

按照你方的要求，我方将签署好的确认书复本寄送给你方。我方已经通过中国银行开具了以你方为受益人的信用证，该信用证完全符合所规定的条件及出货要求。两份文件均随信附上，请查收。

我方希望这次合作能够进一步深化我们之间的合作关系。

DEL公司 谨上

读书笔记

范例 9 | 感谢介绍客户

Dear Mr. James,

Thank you for introducing ABC Company to us. The establishment of the new business relationship with such a large company helped to increase our sales greatly.

Last week, we signed a contract with the director of ABC Company in a comfortable atmosphere. Mr. Smith held you in high regard and was particularly interested in our products designed for the U.S. market. We look forward to providing them with the finest and most cost effective services so that they will never feel regretful to cooperate with us.

We owe you the greatest debt of gratitude.

Yours sincerely,

Lily Chen

FET Company

亲爱的詹姆斯先生：

感谢您将ABC公司介绍给我们。和这家大公司建立新的贸易关系使我们的业务量大增。

上周，我们在友好的气氛中和ABC公司的总裁签订了一份合同。史密斯先生对您进行了高度评价。他对我们针对美国市场设计的产品尤其感兴趣。我们期望能为他们公司提供最优质高效的服务，让他们不会为与我们的合作感到后悔。

我们向您表示由衷的感谢。

FET公司

陈莉莉 敬上

读书笔记

邮件回复 *Reply*

Dear Ms. Chen,

I am very happy to hear that you have successfully established a cooperative business relationship with ABC Company and that you newly signed a contract with them. I always appreciate your company because you have a strong sense of social responsibility and I think ABC Company has also perceived this. You know they never did business with small companies. I hope both of you will benefit from your cooperation.

Yours truly,

Tom James

亲爱的陈女士：

很高兴听说你们成功地与ABC公司建立了合作贸易关系，以及你们刚同他们签订合约的消息。我一直都很欣赏贵公司，因为你们有很强的社会责任感。我想ABC公司也认识到了这一点，要知道他们从来没有与小公司做过生意。我希望你们双方都能从合作中受益。

汤姆·詹姆斯 谨上

读书笔记

范例 10 | 感谢提供样品

Dear Sirs,

We are writing to acknowledge receipt of the sample of lady shaver CD 2215. We really appreciate your prompt attention to our requirement and quick delivery of the sample.

We have examined the sample carefully and are satisfied with its quality and design, although it is a little different from the picture in the catalogue you sent to us. We think this model will meet the demands in this market. But we also find that the price you quoted is too high. Provided that your modified price is attractive, we will place a large order with you.

We appreciate this chance to cooperate with you and hope your satisfying response.

Linda Brown

BBT Company

尊敬的先生：

我方收到了型号为CD2215的女用剃毛刀样品。十分感谢你方对我方要求的立刻关照和样品的快速配送。

我们仔细地研究了送来的样品，对其品质和设计都十分满意，虽然它与你们之前寄送的产品目录上的图片稍有出入。我方认为这种型号符合本地市场的需求。但是我方同时也发现你方的报价过高。如果你方的修改价格具有吸引力，我方将会下一张大数目订单。

我方很珍惜和你方合作的机会，希望你方能对我方的建议做出令人满意的答复。

BBT公司

琳达 · 布朗 谨上

读书笔记

邮件回复 *Reply*

Dear Ms. Brown,

We are happy to hear that you are satisfied with our sample. Lady shaver CD2215 is a new model launched recently. When designing this model, we took American women's needs into consideration, so we have confidence that it will enjoy a promising market in America.

Considering this is the first cooperation between us, we are willing to give you a 5% discount on the condition that your order reaches the amount of $30, 000.

If you have further questions, please feel free to contact us.

Yours sincerely,

Tom Chen

GFI Company

亲爱的布朗女士：

我们很高兴听说你方对我们的样品感到满意。CD2215号女用剃毛刀是我们最近发布的一款新型号产品。我们在设计这款产品时，就考虑过美国女性的需求。因此，我们相信这款产品一定会在美国拥有广阔的市场前景。

考虑到这是我方与你方的首次合作，我们愿意给予你方5%的折扣，前提是你方的订单额不少于30000美元。

若你方还有进一步的问题，请随时与我方联络。

GFI公司

汤姆陈 敬上

读书笔记

范例 11 | 感谢陪伴

Dear Grace,

I'm writing to tell you that I've got home now. I wish to express my gratitude to you for the wonderful holiday I spent with your family members. During the holiday, you taught me how to swim, boat and fish. I really appreciate your taking time off work to show me around so many places.

Surely, I've spent a happy and unforgettable vacation. Thanks again.

I hope you will be going to visit us sometime. Let's keep in touch.

Truly yours,

Henry

亲爱的格瑞丝：

这封信是告诉你我已经回到家了。我想向你表示感谢，因为我与你和你的家人共同度过了一个非常棒的假期。假期中，你教会我游泳、划船和钓鱼。我真的很感激你从繁忙的工作中抽出时间陪我四处游览，参观了那么多地方。

当然，这个假期愉快而难忘。再次表示感谢。

希望你也能有机会来我们这里玩。我们保持联络！

亨利 谨上

邮件回复 *Reply*

Dear Henry,

I'm much honored to be able to accompany you in the rare holiday of your busy time. My wife likes your humorous personality very much. She said she would prepare delicious food waiting for you next time you come to my home.

After a busy work, I will take my wife to visit you and have a look at your beautiful city. I think it will certainly be a pleasant holiday.

Let us keep in touch with each other closely to keep our friendship.

Truly yours,

Grace

亲爱的亨利：

能陪伴你度过忙碌工作之余难得的假期，我十分荣幸。我的妻子非常喜欢你幽默风趣的性格，她说她会为你准备好丰盛的食物等着你下次的到来。

在忙碌的工作结束后，我一定会带着我的妻子去拜访你，游览你所在的那座美丽的城市，我想那肯定将是一段轻松愉快的假期。

你在闲暇时要多与我联系，以便保持我们老朋友的情意！

你的朋友

格瑞丝

范例 12 | 感谢慰问

Dear Diana,

I shall always remember with gratitude the e-mail you sent me when you knew of Jane's death. No one but you knew my sister so well and loved her as her own family did. Only you could write that letter. It brought me comfort, Diana, when I needed it badly.

Thank you from the bottom of my heart for your e-mail and for your much kindness to Jane during her long illness.

Affectionately,

Elizabeth

亲爱的戴安娜：

我永远不能忘记当你得知珍去世后，发给我的那封电子邮件。没有人能像你那样了解我的姐姐，你就像家人一样爱她。只有你能写出那样的慰问信来。戴安娜，当我急需安慰时，这封信给我带来了慰藉。

我从心底感谢你，感谢你的来信，感谢你在珍漫长的患病期间给予她的善意帮助。

你亲爱的

伊丽莎白

邮件回复 *Reply*

Dear Elizabeth,

I am very happy that my E-mail can help you. I am very sorry for Jane's death. As Jane's friend, accompanying her through those difficult days is what I should do. We cannot believe Jane's death, but we still have to live on. I hope you can come out from the pain as soon as possible and live happily every day. That is also what your sister wants to see. I wish you happy every day.

Affectionately,

Diana

亲爱的伊丽莎白：

很高兴我的信能够帮助你。对于珍的离去我也感到很难过。作为珍的朋友，陪她度过那段艰难的日子是我应该做的。珍的去世是我们都不想接受的，但是我们还是要生活下去，希望你能尽快从伤痛中走出来，开心的过每一天，那也将是你姐姐愿意看到的，祝你每天都开心。

你亲爱的

戴安娜

范例 13 | 感谢来信

Dear Alice,

I'm very pleased to receive your letter asking me about my condition. Your letter gives me a lot of comfort; it reminds me of you as a good friend by my side.

Recently I have a lot of things to do, like moving to a new house and doing the housework, so I had no enough time to have a rest, and I was sick. But the doctor said it was nothing, just needed a good rest and something full of nutrition. Now I feel better, especially after receiving your letter. I hope you can take care of your body, and keep a happy mood.

Thank you for your concern. Wish you all the best.

Yours sincerely,

Anna

亲爱的爱丽丝：

我很高兴收到你的来信询问我的病情。你的来信给了我很大的安慰，它提醒我有你这样一个好朋友在我身边。

最近由于事情比较多，又要忙着搬家，又要做家务，没有足够的休息时间。所以就病倒了，但是医生说没什么大的问题，只是需要多休息，补充营养。现在我已经感觉好多了，尤其是收到你的来信后。希望你也注意身体，保持心情愉快。

谢谢你的关心。希望你一切顺利。

安娜 谨上

邮件回复 *Reply*

Dear Anna,

You are my best friend, and I just did what a friend should do. I am glad to know my letter gives you so much encouragement. I hope you can recover soon.

Best wishes!

Yours sincerely,

Alice

亲爱的安娜：

你是我最重要的朋友。关心你是作为朋友应该做的事情。很高兴我的信能给你这么大的鼓励。希望你早日恢复健康。

祝好！

爱丽丝 谨上

范例 14 | 感谢帮助

Dear Alice,

Thank you for helping me find so much information I need. You also have a lot of things to do. Taking you so much time, I feel so sorry to ask you to help me find the materials that I was badly in need of. I feel lucky to have a friend like you who can always give me help in time to solve my problems. You are really a warm-hearted and kind person. Thanks to your materials, I can finish my report very well.

Thank you very much!

Yours sincerely,

Anna

亲爱的爱丽丝：

非常感谢你帮我找了那么多我需要的资料。我知道你也有很多事情要做，让你花时间帮我找资料实在不好意思。很庆幸我有你这样一个朋友，在我有困难的时候能够及时地给我帮助。你真是一个热心、善良的人。多亏了你的资料，我才能更好地完成我的报告。

非常感谢你！

安娜 谨上

邮件回复 *Reply*

Dear Anna,

I am so glad that these materials can help you finish your report. We are friends and we are supposed to help each other. I think if I need your help, you will also help me immediately.

Best wishes!

Yours sincerely,

Alice

亲爱的安娜：

我很高兴这些资料能够对你有所帮助。我们是朋友，互相帮助是应该的。我想要是我有事情需要你的帮助，你同样也会帮助我的。

祝好！

爱丽丝 谨上

范例 15 | 感谢合作

Dear Alice,

Our project is finally finished. Thanks to you, we can finish it so quickly. I'm glad to have you to be my partner. You're very excellent, and there are a lot of people who want to ask you to be their partner, but finally you chose me. In this process, you gave me a lot of help and care. Because of you, this project can be finished so smoothly.

Thank you for your contribution to this cooperation. I hope there will be more opportunities to cooperate. Thank you very much.

I wish you all the best!

Yours sincerely,

Anna

亲爱的爱丽丝：

我们的项目终于完成了。多亏了你，我们才能这么快地完成。我真庆幸能有你这个合作伙伴。你很优秀，有很多人都想要找你当他们的合作伙伴，但是最后你却选择了我。在这个过程中，你给了我很大的帮助和关心。因为有你，才能使得这个项目能够这么顺利地完成。

我非常感谢你能够促成这次的合作。希望以后有更多的机会合作。非常感谢。

祝你一切顺利！

安娜 谨上

邮件回复 *Reply*

Dear Anna,

I am very happy to receive your letter, and thank you for your praise. I think you are a very excellent person who is worthy to cooperate with. In this project, I learned a lot from you. I also hope we can have another opportunity to cooperate again.

Best wishes!

Yours sincerely,

Alice

亲爱的安娜：

收到你的来信我很高兴，谢谢你对我的赞美。我觉得你是一个非常值得合作的人。你也是一个非常优秀的合作伙伴。这次的项目，我从你身上学到很多。我也希望能有机会再次合作。

祝好！

爱丽丝 谨上

范例 16 | 感谢赠送礼品

Dear Alice,

I want to thank you for the flowers you gave me. You know recently I have been upset about life and work. But when I look at them, I feel very comfortable and happy. They remind me that I have such a good friend like you who always help me come out of the frustration. They cheer me up and give me the power. Thank you very much, my dear friend.

Best wishes!

Yours sincerely,

Anna

亲爱的爱丽丝：

我想要谢谢你送我花。你知道最近我对生活和工作都很沮丧。但是每当我看着它们的时候，总是能让我感到舒服和开心。它们提醒着我，我有像你这样的朋友在我身边，经常帮助我走出沮丧。它们让我振奋起来，给我力量。真的非常感谢你，我亲爱的朋友。

祝好！

安娜 谨上

邮件回复 *Reply*

Dear Anna,

I'm glad my flowers could give you so much comfort. I know recently your mood is not very good, and you also have a lot of things to do. I want to do something for you. I think these flowers will make you feel my concern.

Wish you all good!

Yours sincerely,

Alice

亲爱的安娜：

我很高兴我的花能给你这么大的安慰。我知道最近你的心情不是很好，又有很多事情要做。我很想为你做点什么。我想这些花能够让你感受到我的关心。

希望你一切都好！

爱丽丝 谨上

Unit 7 邀请篇

（1）如何写

a）直接说明为何邀请对方，并希望对方能来；

b）写明活动的时间、地点等要素，能够让对方能够事先安排时间；

c）衷心地希望对方能够来参加，表达自己的感谢和祝福。

（2）实用例句

a）I am writing to invite you to come for a luncheon with my family. And I hope you can come.

我写信是想邀请你参加我们家的午宴。我希望你能来。

b）Will you have a dinner with me and my wife to celebrate the success of the project?

你能来我家和我与我的妻子一起吃个晚饭，庆祝这个项目的成功吗？

c）Bob and I will give a party and we wish you can come to have fun with us. It will start at 18:00 on Sunday night. Looking forward to seeing you!

鲍勃和我将会举行一个派对，我们希望你能来玩。聚会将在周日晚上18:00开始。期待见到你。

d）If it is convenient for you, would you like to join in the party we will hold on Saturday night at 18:00? I really hope you can come.

如果你方便的话，希望你能来参加我们周六晚上18:00举行的派对。我真的非常希望你能来。

e）Tomorrow is my birthday and I want to ask you to come to my house to have the party. It will start at 9 a.m. on Sunday.

明天是我的生日，我想邀请你来我家参加我的生日派对。派对将会在周日早上9:00开始。

f）I will be happy if you can come to my house to have dinner next Thursday at 16:00.

如果你能在下周四16:00来我家和我一起吃饭，我会很高兴的。

g）I think it will be of great fun to see a wonderful movie together. Would you like to come with me?

我觉得我们一起去看一部很棒的电影将会很开心。你愿意来吗？

h）This Sunday I will have a wedding banquet in the ××× hotel at 17:00. It would give me so much pleasure if you can come to join us and share the happiness with us.

这个周日我将会在×××酒店，在17:00举行婚宴。如果你能来参加，和我一起分享我的喜悦，我会很高兴的。

i）Thank you for your concern. I am looking forward to seeing you in the party.

谢谢你的关心。我很期待能在聚会上看到你。

j）It's my honor if you can come to join us and best wishes!

如果你能来将是我的荣幸。祝福你！

读书笔记

范例 1 | 邀请共进晚餐

Dear Mr. Li,

We should be much pleased if you and Mrs. Li could dine with us on Friday, March 25, at 7:00 p.m. It will be quite a small party, as we have only asked Mr. and Mrs. Chen, Mr. Zhang and Miss Wang, all our close friends. We will prepare dishes with authentic Sichuan flavor and hope you will like them. We trust you will be disengaged and able to give us the pleasure of your company.

We are looking forward to meeting you.

Yours truly,

Tong Hua

亲爱的李先生：

我们非常荣幸地邀请您携夫人于3月25日，星期五晚上7点来寒舍共聚晚餐。此次聚会人数不多，我们只邀请了陈先生夫妇，张先生和王小姐，他们都是我们的知交。我们准备了地道的四川风味菜肴，希望你们能够喜欢。如能抽空前来，将不胜荣幸。

期待惠临！

童华 谨上

邮件回复 *Reply*

Dear Mr. Tong,

Thank you for your kindness in inviting us for a dinner in your house. We really want to go, but regret that owing to a previous engagement, we shall not be able to accompany you. It is a pity that we will lose a chance to taste Sichuan cuisine.

Any how, thank you for your invitation.

Yours truly,

Li Jun

亲爱的童先生：

感谢您盛情邀请我们到府上共聚晚餐。我们真的很想前往，但是因为之前已有其他预约不能如愿，恐怕没有办法陪伴你们。真是可惜我们错过了品尝四川美食的机会。

无论如何，我们感谢你们的邀请。

李俊 谨上

范例 2 | 邀请参加访问

Dear Mr. Johnson,

It's our great honor to invite you to visit our company in April, 2020. This visit will provide an opportunity for you to make a better understanding of our marketing issues, and to discuss about our future business cooperation in detail.

Since our company is one of your distributors in China, and has been making great progresses in promoting and selling your products, we believe this visit will be of great benefit to our future business cooperation.

Please use this invitation letter to apply for your visa to China.

We are all looking forward to seeing you soon, and should you have any questions, please feel free to inform me.

Yours truly,

Lu Feng

DDT Company

亲爱的约翰逊先生：

我们非常荣幸地邀请您于2020年4月访问我们的公司。通过这次访问，您将有机会更好地了解我公司的销售计划，并就将来的贸易合作与我们进行详细的交流。

作为你们在中国的主要分销商之一，我们公司一直在推广与销售你们的产品方面取得巨大的成绩，我们相信这次访问将有利于我们将来的贸易合作。

请以这封邀请函作为您申请中国签证的依据。

我们期待早日见到您。如果你还有问题，请随时告知我。

DDT公司

陆丰 敬上

读书笔记

邮件回复 Reply

Dear Mr. Lu,

Thank you for your kindness in inviting me to your company. I have been eager to visit China, which is universally well-known for its beautiful scenery and culture.

I want to take this chance to communicate with you, since you made great contributions to the promotion and sale of our products in Chinese market. I agree that we will both benefit from this visit.

I will let you know the date of my arrival if it is fixed.

Yours truly,

Tom Johnson

FOB Company

亲爱的陆先生：

感谢您盛情邀请我访问贵公司。我一直都很期望能够到中国访问，这是一个风景如画、文化灿烂的国度。

我想趁此机会与你们进行交流；你们为我们的产品在中国市场的推广和销售做出了重要贡献。我非常赞同，我们双方都会从这次访问中受益。

一旦我抵达的时间确定下来，我就会告知你的。

FOB公司

汤姆·约翰逊敬上

读书笔记

范例 3 | 邀请参加研讨会

Dear Prof. Smith,

BBG Company has pleasure in informing you that we will host a seminar on World Water Pollution Control on May 16, 2020, in Wuhan International Exhibition Center, Wuhan, China. You are one of the top experts in the field and we think you must be interested in the conference. We will provide funds for your travel and per diem expenses. We hope that you will be able to attend. Please indicate acceptance by email within the next few days.

We are looking forward to your attendance.

Yours sincerely,

Lu Feng

BBG Company

尊敬的史密斯教授：

BBG公司很荣幸地通知您我们将于2020年5月16日在中国武汉国际会展中心举办世界水污染控制研讨会。您是这一领域的顶级专家，我们想您一定会对这次会议感兴趣的。我们提供专项资金，承担你的旅行及日支费用。我们希望您能参加。请您在最近几天通过电邮的方式告知我们您是否接受我们的邀请。

我们期待您与会。

BBG公司

陆丰 敬上

邮件回复 *Reply*

Dear Mr. Lu,

Thank you for your invitation to the World Water Pollution Control Conference on May 16, 2020, in Wuhan International Exhibition Center, Wuhan, China. I accept it with pleasure and would be very happy to contribute to the discussion. You arc so kind to provide the fund for travel and accommodation. I will begin to make some preparations for the trip and inform you of the date of my arrival once it is fixed.

Yours truly,

Tom Smith

亲爱的陆先生：

感谢您邀请我参加2020年5月16日在中国武汉国际会展中心举办世界水污染控制会议。我欣然应邀，并且很高兴能为会议讨论做出贡献。你们提供旅费及食宿，真是太周到了。我将开始为此次行程做准备，一旦抵达日期确定，我会通知你们。

汤姆 · 史密斯 谨上

范例 4｜邀请参加新闻发布会

Dear Sir or Madam:

Approved by the State Council of P.R. China and co-organized by China Environmental Protection Association (CEPA), Hubei Association of Environmental Protection Industry (HAEPI), China Environmental Science Press, Water Pollution Institute of Wuhan University, BBG Company, and Wuhan Municipal Government, the World Water Pollution Control Conference will be held on May 16, 2020.

To facilitate your better understanding of the conference, a press conference will be held in Wuhan International Exhibition Center, at 9:00–10:00 a.m., on April 29, 2020.

Please refer to *www.wwpcc.org* for further information of the World Water Pollution Control Conference.

Please confirm whether you would attend the press conference by emailing us the confirming note (see attached). We will send the formal invitation letter upon receipt of your confirming note.

Contact Persons: Zhou Liyan, Song Bing

Tel: 027-82080090, 82078904

Email: wwpcc@hotmail.com

女士们，先生们：

经中华人民共和国国务院批准，由中国环境保护协会（CEPA）、湖北环境保护产业协会（HAEPI）、中国环境科学出版社、武汉大学水污染研究所、BBG公司及武汉市政府共同举办，世界水污染控制会议将于2020年5月16日举行。

2020年4月29日上午9：00—10：00，将在武汉国际会展中心举行新闻发布会，向中外记者介绍此次大会的相关情况。欢迎参加。

了解大会详情，请登录网站：www.wwpcc.org。

能否出席，请电邮确认（见附件）。收到确认出席的回执单后，我们将向您发出正式的邀请函。

联系人：周立言　宋兵

电话:027—82080090,82078904

邮 箱：wwpcc@hotmail.com

邮件回复 *Reply*

Dear Sirs,

Thank you for your invitation to the press conference on April 29, 2020, and we accept it with pleasure. We will send 3 persons to the conference, for their personal data, please see the attached document.

Enclosed please also find the confirmation note.

Wuhan Evening News

尊敬的先生们：

感谢你们邀请我们参加2020年4月29日举办的新闻发布会，我们很高兴地接受邀请。我们将派出3人与会。有关他们的个人资料，请参见附件。

回执单也以附件形式送出。

武汉晚报

读书笔记

范例 5 | 邀请参加周年庆典

Dear Sir or Madam:

We take great pleasure to invite you to our company's 10th anniversary ceremony. We will hold a cocktail party at 3:00–5:00 p.m., on May 8th, 2020, in Shanghai Grand Hotel. We are looking forward to having your company in the party.

Enclosed you will find a formal invitation card.

We would appreciate it if you could confirm your availability at your earliest convenience. Please contact us at 021–53342728.

Yours sincerely,

Zhang ying

BBC Company

亲爱的先生/女士：

我们很荣幸地邀请您参加我公司10周年纪念活动。我们将于2020年5月8日下午3:00~5:00在上海大酒店举行鸡尾酒会。期待您的光临。

附件中请查收正式邀请函一封。

如果您能尽早告知是否赏光，我们将不胜感激。请拨021—53342728联系我们。

BBC公司

张英 敬上

邮件回复 *Reply*

Dear Miss Zhang,

Thank you for your kind invitation to your 10th anniversary ceremony. We accept it with pleasure and enjoy the honor to be with you on that happy event.

We have witnessed how you started and developed in these years and happy to see it has achieved so much. Of course, we will be there, sharing your happiness that day.

Yours sincerely,

Liu Feng

YTY Company

亲爱的张小姐：

感谢您盛情邀请我们参加贵公司10周年庆典活动。我们欣然接受，并且很荣幸能够和你们共度这一欢乐时刻。

我们见证了贵公司的初创和发展，为它所取得的成就感到高兴。当然，我们会在那天和你们一起分享快乐。

YTY 公司

刘峰 敬上

范例 6 | 邀请担任发言人

Dear Mr. Smith,

We are going to have a press conference at Shanghai Grand Hotel at 9:00-11:00, next Friday morning, May 14, 2020. We organize it to launch a new product model recently developed by our company. We know that you are a spokesman with good reputation and you are quite familiar with our field. Could we have the honor to invite you to speak in our conference? For the detailed information about the product in question, and the press conference, please refer to the attached document. Please confirm whether you will accept our invitation through email.

We will appreciate your prompt attention to our invitation.

Yours sincerely,
Lily Chen
BBC Company

亲爱的史密斯先生：

我们将于2020年5月14日，下个星期五早晨9:00~11:00在上海大酒店举行新闻发布会，发布我公司最近开发的一款新产品。我们知道您是一位享有良好声誉的发言人，并且对我们这一领域了解颇多。我们是否有这个荣幸邀请您担任此次会议的发言人呢？有关该产品及其发布会的情况请参见附件。请您通过电邮方式告知我们是否接受我们的邀约。

如能尽快关照我们的邀请，将不胜感激。

BBC公司
陈莉莉 谨上

邮件回复 *Reply*

Dear Ms. Chen,

Thank you for your invitation to the press conference for your new product. I have studied the enclosed documents and I am quite interested in it. It is my honor to speak for such a renowned company.

Please send me a formal invitation so that I can apply for the visa to China.

Yours sincerely,
Tom Smith

亲爱的陈女士：

感谢贵公司邀请我参加你们的新产品发布会。我已经研读了你们随信附上的文件，并且对发布会非常感兴趣。我很荣幸能够代表这样一家著名的公司发言。

请给我寄送一份正式的邀请函，以便我申请去中国的签证。

汤姆·史密斯 谨上

范例 7｜邀请出席活动

Dear Mr. Yang,

This year is the 110th anniversary of the establishment of Wuhan University. We are planning to celebrate the event with an alumni reunion at the Academic Exchange Center of our school at 9:00–11:00 a.m. on Sunday, May 16, 2020. It is our honor to have your company in the party. And we will appreciate it if you can address the party for about 15 minutes.

Please indicate your availability or inability to attend the party as soon as possible.

Yours sincerely,

Lu Fen

Wuhan University

亲爱的杨先生：

今年是武汉大学建校110周年。我们正在筹备一个校友聚会以兹庆贺。聚会定于2020年5月16日，星期天上午9:00~11:00在我校学术交流中心举行。如能出席，不胜荣幸。如果您能够做一个15分钟左右的致辞我们将感激不尽。

请尽快告知我们您是否能出席。

武汉大学

陆芬 敬上

邮件回复 *Reply*

Dear Ms. Lu,

Thank you for your kind invitation to the celebration of the 110th anniversary of the establishment of my alma mater. I shall look forward with pleasure to attending the event and meeting my old schoolfellows. As to your asking me to address the party, I accept the task with pleasure.

Yours sincerely,

Yang Yang

亲爱的陆女士：

感谢您盛情邀请我参加母校110年华诞庆典。我非常期待参加庆祝活动，并且有机会见到校友。您要求我在会上致辞，我欣然接受。

杨扬 谨上

范例 8 | 邀请进行合作

Dear Sir or Madam:

Being specialized in the trade of clothes and relative goods, we express our desire to trade with you in this line. We are a leading exporter of casual wear in China and have earned a good reputation in European and American markets.

On the basis of equality, mutual benefit and the exchange of needed goods, we are looking forward to establishing a cooperative business partnership with you. If you are interested in this idea, you are welcomed to visit our company to get a better understanding of it.

Please inform us of your itinerary so as to facilitate our arrangements in advance.

Please feel free to ask any question if there is anything you are particularly interested in.

Looking forward to your reply.

Yours faithfully ,

Zhang Dan

BBE Company

尊敬的先生/女士：

作为专业的服装和相关产品的贸易公司，我们希望在此方面与你们开展合作。我们是中国最大的休闲服饰出口商，在欧美市场上赢得了较好的声誉。

我们期望在平等互利、互通有无的基础上与你们发展贸易合作关系。如果你们对此抱有兴趣，欢迎访问我公司，以便获得更全面的了解。

请尽早通知我们你们的日程安排，便于我们提前安排接待工作。

如果有任何问题，请尽管向我们询问。

期待你们的回复。

BBE公司

张丹 敬上

邮件回复 Reply

Dear Ms. Zhang,

We acknowledge receipt of your letter dated on May 18th, 2020. We are interested in your proposal that we establish a business partnership. We want to know more about your company, so we are considering sending a delegation to visit your company. We will inform you of the number of the delegation members and the date of their arrival in advance.

Yours sincerely,

Zhu Tong

FGT Company

亲爱的张女士：

你们2020年5月18日的来信已收到。我们对于你们建立合作伙伴关系的提议很感兴趣。我们想要更加详细地了解贵公司，正在考虑派遣代表团访问贵公司。我们将会提前告知你们有关代表团的人数和抵达日期的情况。

FGT公司

朱彤 谨上

读书笔记

范例 9｜接受邀请

Dear Mr. Yang,

Thank you for your letter of March 28, inviting our corporation to participate in the 2020 International Fair. We are very pleased to accept and will plan to display our electrical appliances as we did in previous years.

Mr. Li will be in your city from May 5 to 10 to make specific arrangements and would very much appreciate your assistance.

Yours faithfully,

Zhang Bo

ABC Company

尊敬的杨先生：

感谢3月28日来信邀请我公司参加2020国际商品交易会。我们乐于参加并计划展示我们前几年生产的电子设备。

李先生将于5月5日至10日去你市做具体安排，非常感谢您的协助。

ABC公司

张波 敬上

邮件回复 *Reply*

Dear Mr. Zhang,

We have received your confirmation to participate in the 2020 International Fair, and thank you for your support.

You will find that some of your business partners will also be present in the Fair. We believe that this will be a good chance for you to communicate with each other.

Yours faithfully,

Yang Yang

尊敬的张先生，

我们收到了你们关于参加2020国际商品交易会的确认函，感谢你们的支持。

你们将会发现你们一些贸易伙伴也会到场。我们相信这会是一个促进彼此交流的良好契机。

杨扬 敬上

范例 10 | 拒绝邀请

Dear Mr. Brown,

Thank you very much for your kindness in asking us to attend your opening ceremony, but I regret very much that I will not be able to go there as I already have an important previous engagement that day.

I send our congratulations and best wishes to you and will be together with you in spirit on this happy event.

Yours sincerely,

Mark Wang

亲爱的布朗先生：

非常感谢你盛情邀请我参加贵公司的开业典礼，但我很遗憾不能前往，因为那天我已经有一个重要的之前就订好的约会。

我谨献上我们的祝贺及真诚的祝福；在这欢乐的时刻，我的心将与你们同在。

王马克 谨上

邮件回复 *Reply*

Dear Mark,

It is a pity not to have your company in my opening ceremony.

I meant to take this chance to get together with you; we have not seen each other for about a year. I also want to thank your for your supporting in my hard times. I can achieve nothing without you, not to say owning a company of my own. I have been looking forward to enjoying this happy moment with you.

Anyhow, I understand you; you always keep your promise. That is why I appreciate you.

Yours truly,

White Brown

亲爱的马克：

很遗憾开业那天你不能来。

我原本打算借此机会和你聚一聚，我们有将近一年都没有见面了。我还想对你在我困难的日子里向我伸出援手表示感谢。没有你，我不可能取得任何成功，更别说会拥有自己的公司了。我一直期盼着能与你共聚这一欢乐时刻。

不管怎么样，我理解你，你是一个恪守承诺的人。这也是我欣赏你的地方。

怀特 · 布朗 谨上

范例 11 | 取消邀请

Dear Mr. and Mrs. Lin,

We regret that, owing to some unseen circumstances, we are obliged to recall our invitation for this Saturday, May 20th.

We meant to get together and enjoy a happy night in my house, since we haven't met each other for so long. However, unfortunately, our daughter, Annie, broke her leg yesterday and we have to take care of her in hospital. It is impossible for us to hold a party in this situation.

We apologize for the inconvenience we may bring to you. And we are looking forward to receiving you in the future occasions.

Yours truly,

White Brown

亲爱的林先生、林太太：

由于某些无法预料的情况，我们很遗憾不得不取消原定于5月20日本周六的邀请。

我们原本准备在我家共度一个愉快的夜晚；我们已经有那么长时间都没有见面了。然而不幸的是，我们的女儿安妮昨天摔断了腿，我们不得不到医院护理她。在这种情况下，我们不能举办派对了。

我们为给你们带来的不便表示道歉。希望以后有机会能够招待你们。

怀特·布朗 敬上

邮件回复 *Reply*

Dear Mr. and Mrs. Brown,

We are sorry to hear that Annie broke her leg. Poor Annie!

We hope she didn't hurt seriously. We are going to visit her this Saturday. Could you please tell us which hospital she is staying in?

Please give Annie our best wishes.

Yours sincerely,

Lin Feng

亲爱的布朗先生、布朗太太：

我们很抱歉听说安妮摔断了腿。可怜的安妮！

我们希望她伤得不严重。本周六我们会去看她。你们能否告诉我们她现在住在哪家医院？

请转达给安妮我们最美好的祝愿。

林峰 敬上

范例 12 | 邀请参加聚会

Dear Lynn,

I have good news to tell you. Bill and I had moved to Chaoyang District, which I had told you last time. We liked it very much. We would like to invite all of our friends to come to our new home for a housewarming party.

Please join us at 17:00 p.m. on Sunday, March 28, 2020. Directions are enclosed.

We hope you and your wife will be able to attend on time.

Yours truly,

Laura

亲爱的林恩：

我有个高兴的事要告诉你，那就是最近比尔和我已经搬到了朝阳区，就是上次我给你说的那里，我们都很喜欢，并且我们想邀请所有的朋友来我们的新家参加乔迁庆宴。

时间就定在这个星期日，即2020年3月28日下午五点，附地图。

希望您和您太太都能够准时来参加。

劳拉谨上

邮件回复 *Reply*

Dear Laura,

Hearing this news, I am also very happy for you. I know you are very satisfied with that village, and the environment is really good. The traffic is so convenient that you can save a lot of time. It is near the school for children. I think it very good to live there. We will attend your party on time.

Yours,

Lynn

亲爱的劳拉：

听到这个消息，我也很替你们开心。我知道你们都很中意那个小区，小区的环境的确不错，交通也很方便，以后你上下班就省掉很多时间了，离孩子学校也近，住那儿真好。我们一定会准时参加的。

林恩谨上

范例 13 | 邀请参加婚礼

Dear John,

On Labor Day, May 1, at ten o'clock a.m., Leo and I are holding wedding ceremony. We are getting married at St. Peter', that quiet little church which you know — at 5 Zhongguancun Street.

We have sent the invitation card to you. It would not be perfect if you were absent. There will be an informal reception in the church parlor and afterwards we want you be there, too.

Affectionately yours,

Cathy

亲爱的约翰：

劳动节当天，5月1日上午10点，我和里尔将举行结婚仪式。我们选在圣彼得那座宁静的小教堂里举行，你知道它的地址——中关村大街5号。

我们给你寄了喜帖，如果你不在场，这场婚礼就显得不那么完美。我们还设了便宴，婚礼后在接待室举行，我们同样希望你能光临。

凯西 谨上

邮件回复 *Reply*

Dear Cathy,

Congratulations. The day of your wedding finally comes. I could imagine how excited and happy you are. We are the witnesses of your love all the time. I believe that god will not be ill-treated to those who spares no effort to pursuit of happiness. You are going to get what you want. I will attend your wedding.

Yours sincerely,

John

亲爱的凯西：

恭喜你，这一天终于来临，我能想象你有多么激动和幸福。这一路上，我们见证着你们的爱情。相信上天不会亏待每个用心努力追求幸福的女孩，你也一定会得到自己想要的幸福。我一定会准时参加的。

约翰 谨上

范例 14 | 邀请参加生日聚会

Dear Louise,

I sincerely invite you to join my birthday party!

It's my 18th birthday. I am going to have a huge birthday cake and we have prepared various kinds of interesting games! Please call me to let me know if you can come. If the answer is yes, don't forget to bring me a beautiful present!

The date: Sunday, April 4, from 5 to 8 p.m.

P.S.: Please tell your parents that there will be a dance party for the grownups, too!

Yours sincerely,

Hannah

亲爱的路易丝：

我真诚地邀请你来参加我的生日聚会！

这是我18岁生日。我将有一个巨大的生日蛋糕，而且准备了好多有趣的游戏！请打电话告诉我你来不来。如果你愿意前来的话，别忘了带给我一份漂亮的礼物哦！

时间：星期日，4月4日，下午5点到8点。

附言：请告诉你的父母，我们也为大人准备了舞会！

汉娜 谨上

邮件回复 *Reply*

Dear Hannah,

Wish you happy birthday in advance. The time passed quickly, so you have grown into a pretty, sensible girl. As your friend, I can feel your youth and vitality all the time. I prepared a gift for you; I hope you'll like it. It's a secret. I will attend the party on time, and let us sing songs together for your birthday.

Yours

Louise

亲爱的汉娜：

提前祝贺你生日快乐，时间过得真快，这么快你也成年了，长成一个漂亮懂事的姑娘，作为你的朋友，我时刻能感受到你身上焕发出来的青春与活力。我给你准备了一份生日礼物，相信你一定会喜欢，暂时就小小保密一下。这个聚会我一定会准时参加，到时让我们一起为你唱生日歌。

路易斯 谨上

范例 15 | 邀请看话剧

Dear Sally,

My husband and I are very pleased to invite you and your husband to see the play. It is scheduled on next Saturday night at seven o'clock, at Qintai Theatre. I also invited several other friends, and I hope we can go after watching the drama, singing karaoke. If you can bring some tapes, I believe this will be a very wonderful evening.

We sincerely hope you will be able to come.

Yours,

Mary

亲爱的萨利：

我与我先生非常高兴地邀请你和你的丈夫前来看话剧。时间定于下个星期六晚上七点，地点位于琴台大剧院。我还邀请了几位别的朋友，并且我希望看完话剧之后我们可以去唱卡拉OK。如果你能带些录像来，我确信这会是一个非常愉快的夜晚。

我们真心希望你们能够前来。

玛丽 谨上

邮件回复 *Reply*

Dear Mary,

Thank you for your invitation, Robin and I will be punctual for the appointment. You still remember that I am very fond of play. I've just learned the drama next Saturday is the one I have been looking for. Robin is fond of singing. Thank you for your thoughtful arrangement. I believe we will have a pleasant weekend. I can't wait to see it.

Yours sincerely,

Sally

亲爱的玛丽：

谢谢你的邀请，我和罗宾一定会准时赴约的。你一定还记得我非常喜欢话剧，我刚得知下周六上映的话剧正是我一直期待的。而罗宾他很喜欢唱歌，感谢你们如此周到的安排。我相信我们一定会度过一个愉悦的周末。想到这我都已经有些迫不及待了。

萨利 谨上

范例 16 | 邀请参加书友会

Dear Doctor Chen,

I am delighted to inform you that you are sincerely invited to participate in the book club of Wuhan as our guest. Your round-trip air ticket, accommodations and meal expenses will be subsidized by us. If you are interested in this, please let us know at your earliest convenience.

I am looking forward to seeing you in this conference, and I am sure you will play an important role in the event. If your response is yes, I'll send the relevant information to you.

Yours sincerely,

NS Sponsor

尊敬的陈博士：

很高兴通知您，我们衷心邀请您作为嘉宾，出席我们在武汉举办的书友会。您的往返机票、住宿与餐饮费用将完全由我们支付。如果您有意参加，请在方便时尽早联系我们。

期待在会议上看到您的身影，我确信您会在此次会议中担任重要的角色。如果您答应参加，我会把相关信息寄送给您。

NS 主办者

邮件回复 *Reply*

Dear NS Sponsor,

Thank you for your kind invitation to attend the book club, and deliver a speech at the meeting. I am pleased to accept your invitation. It has always been my favorite way to make friends through book club. In the book club we can make more illustrious friends, and share the joy of books, and obtain knowledge of life. I will attend on time, please remember to send me relevant information to facilitate preparations in advance.

Dr Chen

尊敬的主办者：

感谢你盛情邀请我参加这次书友会，并在会上发言。我很高兴接受你的邀请。以书会友，一直都是我喜欢的交友方式。在这里可以结识更多同道中人，大家一起分享书籍带给我们的欢乐，并从中获取人生认知。我会准时参加，请记得寄给我相关信息，以方便提前准备。

陈博士

范例 17 | 反客为主邀请

Dear Mr. Yang,

With great pleasure I have received your invitation letter to have lunch on Saturday, June, 15.

I would be very happy to have the opportunity of discussing with you on the proposed visit to Beijing by your Minister of Education. I would be even happier if you could let me host the lunch for you at 12:00 on that day in Wangfujing Grand Hotel. I am sure you will give me your consent since you are in Beijing and I should be the host.

I am looking forward to the pleasure of meeting you on Saturday at 12:00 in the lobby of Wangfujing Grand Hotel.

With my best regards,

Hanna Wei

尊敬的杨先生：

收到关于您希望我参加六月十五日（星期六）午宴的邀请信，我非常高兴。

我非常高兴有这样一个机会就贵国教育部长计划访问北京一事与您进行讨论，更乐于尽地主之谊，于当天十二点在王府井饭店宴请您。我相信您会给我这个机会，因为您来到了北京，作为东道主的我理应如此。

我期待星期六十二点在北京王府井饭店大厅与您相见。

表示我最诚挚的祝福，

魏汉纳 谨上

邮件回复 *Reply*

Dear Mr.Wei,

Thank you for your invitation. It is kind of you. Having heard that Beijing food is good, I will be punctual for the appointments. I'm glad to take this opportunity to discuss with you about the education and cooperation between our two countries. I believe this will promote the academic cooperation and friendship between the two countries. This has far-reaching significance.

Yours sincerely,

Yang

尊敬的魏先生：

感谢您的邀请，您真是太热情了。早就听说北京菜很不错，我一定会准时赴约。我也很高兴借这个机会和您一起商讨两国教育合作的事情，我相信这对于推进学术合作、促进两国友谊有深远意义。

杨 谨上

范例 18 | 出游邀请

Dear Mary,

The cherry blossoms of Wuhan University is blooming, so Jack and I invite you to see the flowers on Saturday. You know that the cherry blossoms in Wuhan University is very famous. Every year a lot of tourists come here especially for the beautiful cherry blossoms. I think you'll like it. Wuhan University has a long history and a strong Academic atmosphere. Walking in such a beautiful campus, you will get your body and mind relaxed. I am looking forward to your reply.

Yours,

Lily

亲爱的玛丽：

武汉大学的樱花盛开了，因此我和杰克邀请你本周六去武大赏花。你也知道武汉大学的樱花很出名，每年樱花盛开的时候都有很多游客慕名而来，樱花盛开的时候非常漂亮我想你一定会喜欢的，武汉大学也是一个有着悠久历史的大学，有着浓厚的学术氛围，漫步在这样一个美丽的校园，你会从身心上得到放松，期待你的同游。

莉莉 谨上

邮件回复 *Reply*

Dear Lily,

Thank you for your invitation this Saturday. I was too tired these days. It is just a chance to rest myself. You know I like the flowers of cherry blossoms. I have heard that Wuhan University is famous for cherry blossoms. But I have no chance to enjoy it. Your invitation is too exciting. I hope the week end come soon. We will meet at the school gate of the Wuhan University.

Yours sincerely,

Mary

亲爱的莉莉：

谢谢你的邀请，这周六我刚好放假，这段时间太累了也想给自己找个机会休息下，你知道吗，我最喜欢的花就是樱花了，一直都听说武汉大学的樱花很有名却没机会欣赏，这个消息太让人兴奋了，真希望周末快点来临。到时我们在校门口见。

玛丽 谨上

Unit 8 祝贺篇

（1）如何写

a）说明信息来源，开门见山表达自己的祝贺和喜悦；

b）对对方获得的成就做出评价，肯定对方的努力，给予鼓励，也可以提出建议；

c）表达美好的祝愿。

（2）实用例句

a）What exciting news!

真是令人激动的消息！

b）I am so happy to hear this news!

我很高兴听到这个消息！

c）It's the most joyful news I have heard for a long time.

这是我这么长时间来听到的最令人高兴的消息。

d）Congratulations and best wishes to you.

祝贺你，祝你一切都好。

e）You have done a good job, and I am so proud of you.

你做得很好，我为你自豪。

f）You have paid a lot of efforts and you deserve it.

你付出了很多努力，你值得拥有。

g）I will always be there for you. Keep going.

我将永远在你身边支持你，继续努力。

h）I believe that you will make more achievements in your career.

我相信你的事业将会有更多成就。

i）Wish you everything goes well!

祝你一切顺利！

范例 1 | 祝贺同事生日

Dear Sam,

This is your first birthday after you came to the company. Happy birthday to you! You make our life in the office more harmonious and peaceful with your kindheartedness and passion. We have developed good friendship and I look forward to enjoying it for years to come.

May you enjoy a happy birthday, a successful career and a happy family!

Yours sincerely,

Tom Hill

亲爱的萨姆：

这是你来到公司后的第一个生日，祝你生日快乐！因为你的善良和热情，我们的工作生活变得更加和谐安宁。我们已经建立起了深厚的友谊，我也盼望在将来的日子里能享受这份友谊。

希望你度过一个快乐的生日，祝你工作顺利，家庭幸福！

汤姆·希尔 敬上

邮件回复 *Reply*

Dear Tom,

Many thanks for your good wishes. I am very delightful to invite you and the other colleagues to come to my house for my birthday party at 6:30 tomorrow evening.

I'm looking forward to your company!

Yours sincerely,

Sam Clarkson

亲爱的汤姆：

十分感谢你对我的生日祝福，我很高兴邀请你和其他同事于明天晚上六点半来我家参加我的生日派对。

我期待你的到来！

萨姆·克拉克森 敬上

范例 2 | 祝贺领导生日

Dear Mr. Steve,

Congratulations on your 50th birthday. This is a special and important day for you and we would like to express our sincerest greetings.

To achieve better performance, we will pull together and help each other sincerely as usual.

With affectionate birthday wishes.

Yours faithfully,

K&W Company

尊敬的史蒂夫先生：

祝您50岁生日快乐！对您来说，今天是一个特殊而又重要的日子，在这个特别的时刻，我们想献上我们最真诚的祝福。

为给公司带来更好的业绩，我们会如往常一样齐心合力，真诚互助。

送上我美好的生日祝福。

K&W公司员工 谨上

邮件回复 *Reply*

Dear all,

Thank you for your greetings.

I will hold a party in the canteen at 6:00–8:00 p.m. this Friday. Everyone will be welcomed to enjoy a happy night with me.

I am looking forward to seeing you all.

Yours sincerely,

John Steve

各位同仁：

感谢大家的问候。

我将于本周五晚上6:00~8:00在公司餐厅举办派对，诚邀各位与我共度一个愉快的夜晚。

期盼各位光临。

约翰 · 史蒂夫 谨上

范例 3 | 祝贺乔迁

Dear Shelly,

I'm so glad to hear that you have a house of your own eventually. What a wonderful thing to live in a house with such nice surroundings. Thanks for telling me your new address.

It's great to have a chance to call at your new house. I have sent you a basket of flowers as a token of my hearty congratulations on changing your residence. I hope you will like it and wish everything goes well!

Yours sincerely,

Laura

亲爱的谢莉：

你终于有了自己的房子，我衷心地为你感到高兴。在周围环境这么优美的地方开始新生活，是多么美好的一件事啊！谢谢你告诉我你新房子地址。

我很高兴有机会去你的新家做客。我寄给你一篮鲜花，希望你会喜欢。祝你一切顺利！

真诚的

劳拉

邮件回复 *Reply*

Dear Laura,

Thank you for taking time to congratulate me on entering a new house. You can imagine how happy I am to live in my own house. I am planning to have a party after I have settled everything. I will invite some close friend like you to celebrate this happy event in my life.

I am looking forward to seeing you.

Yours sincerely,

Shelly

亲爱的劳拉：

感谢你恭贺我乔迁。你可以想象我是多么高兴能住在自己的房子里啊。我计划在一切安顿好之后举办一个派对。我会邀请几个像你一样的密友一起庆祝这件人生乐事。

期待你的光临。

谢莉 敬上

范例 4 | 祝贺公司开业

Dear Kevin,

Please accept our sincerest congratulations on the establishment of your company. There is a long way to go, we wish you every success in the complicated domestic market. Should there be any way in which we can give you a hand, please do not hesitate to contact me directly.

Yours sincerely,

Rick

亲爱的凯文：

对贵公司的开业，特此献上最热烈的祝贺。还有很长一段路要走，我们预祝贵公司在复杂的国内市场上能创造不凡的业绩。如果需要我公司帮忙，请直接联系我们。

里克 敬上

邮件回复 *Reply*

Dear Rick,

Thank you for taking the time to congratulate us on the establishment of our company. This would not have been possible without the unyielding support from my old friends like you. I will spare no effort to make it successful and prosperous.

Yours sincerely,

Keven

亲爱的里克：

感谢您对我们公司开业表示祝贺。没有像您一样的老朋友坚定的支持，这是不可能的。我会不遗余力地使公司发展繁荣。

凯文 敬上

范例 5 | 祝贺职位晋升

Dear Matt,

I know how happy you must be at the news of your promotion to Sales Manager. I am cheerful that your efforts you've done have been recognized and appreciated. The new title is well deserved. Congratulations!

I would also like to take the opportunity to express my sincere thanks for your kind help and support. I wish you make better achievements in your new position.

Yours sincerely,

Chris

亲爱的马特：

我知道你在得知你晋升营业部经理的消息之后一定很高兴。我为你在工作上所付出的努力被认可、欣赏而感到开心。你得此新头衔是当之无愧的。祝贺你！

我也想借此机会对你曾经给予我的帮助和支持表示感谢。我祝愿你在新职位上能取得更好的成就。

克里斯 敬上

邮件回复 *Reply*

Dear Chris,

Thank you for taking the time to congratulate me on my recent promotion. Quite frankly, I know I could not have come this far without the close support and encouragement of friends like you. I will certainly try my best to achieve better achievements as you referred in your letter.

Yours sincerely,

Matt

亲爱的克里斯：

感谢你对我新近晋升的祝贺。老实说，我很清楚如果没有像你一样的朋友的支持和鼓励，我是不可能取得今天的成就的。我当然会像你信中所写的那样尽力取得更好的成绩的。

马特 敬上

范例 6 | 祝贺新公司营业

Dear Director Wang,

It is wonderful to know that your new branch in Zhejiang will open and be ready for business, congratulations!

With your practical experience and proven capability in the business field, I believe your organization will make great success in the near future.

Please accept my kindest congratulations and best wishes.

Yours sincerely,

Tian xin

亲爱的王董事长：

得知贵公司的浙江分公司即将开业，真是好极了！恭喜！

凭您在商界的实战经验和业内公认的能力，我相信贵公司在不久的将来会取得巨大的成功。

请您接受我最诚挚的祝贺和祝愿。

田昕 谨上

邮件回复 *Reply*

Dear Ms. Tian,

Thank you for your congratulations on the establishment of our Zhejiang Branch. This achievement would not have been possible without the outstanding performance of distributors like you.

We are determined to make this year an even bigger one for us all and would like to ask again for your continuing support and cooperation.

Yours sincerely,

Wang Qiang

亲爱的田女士：

感谢您对我们浙江分部营业表示祝贺。这一成绩没有像您一样的分销商的优良表现是不可能的。

我们决心今年取得更大的成绩，我们再次请求您的继续支持和合作。

王强 谨上

范例 7 | 祝贺事业扩大

Dear Jack,

How great it is to know that you have expanded your company. It is so amazing that you have achieved so much on such a short period of time. I suppose this huge success must owe to your strong leadership and the efforts of all the staff.

Please accept my heartiest congratulations and best wishes for your further success.

Yours sincerely,

Mike

亲爱的杰克：

得知贵公司扩大规模的消息，我感到十分高兴。贵公司在这么短时间内取得如此大的成就实在令人惊叹。我想这份巨大的成功归功于你优秀的领导能力和员工的一致努力。

请接受我最衷心的祝贺，并祝愿贵方能取得更大的成功。

迈克 谨上

邮件回复 *Reply*

Dear Mike,

Thank you for taking the time to congratulate us on the expansion of our company. This achievement would not have been possible without the outstanding performance of distributors like you.

We are determined to make this year an even bigger one for us all and would like to again ask for your continuing support and cooperation.

Yours sincerely,

Jack

亲爱的迈克：

感谢您对我们公司扩大规模表示祝贺。这一成绩没有像您一样的经销商的优良表现是不可能实现的。

我们决心今年取得更大的成绩，我们再次请求您的继续支持和合作。

杰克 谨上

范例 8 | 祝贺退休

Dear Mr. Wood,

We've heard the news that you have officially resigned from your role as Chairman of the Board. It has been a great pleasure working under you over the last 20 years. Your excellent leadership and management was pivotal to BYK's growth and success. Over the years, our relationship grew more and more close. After your retirement, you have plenty of time to do what you want to do – traveling, reading, playing golf and spending more time with your family.

All the members of BYK wish you to enjoy your retirement.

Yours faithfully,

All staff of BYK

尊敬的伍德先生：

我们得知您已经正式从董事长的职位上退休辞职了。过去的二十年里，能在您手下工作是一件十分愉快的事情。你卓越的领导才能和管理能力对BYK公司的成长与成功举足轻重。在一起工作的日子里，您和我们员工之间的关系不断加深。在您退休之后，您可以有大把的时间做自己想做的事情，比如旅行、读书、打高尔夫，有更多的时间和家人相处。

我们BYK全体员工祝您幸福快乐。

真诚的

BYK公司全体职员

邮件回复 *Reply*

Dear all,

Thank you for your greetings.

It is a pity that I will be unable to work with you in the future. However, I will never forget the happy days we spent together. I wish you every success in your work and life.

Yours sincerely,

Smith Wood

各位同仁：

感谢大家的问候。

以后不能与大家共事，真是太遗憾了。然而，我不会忘记与你们一起度过的那些美好的日子。我祝愿大家在工作和生活中顺心如意。

史密斯 · 伍德 谨上

范例 9 | 祝贺应聘成功

Dear Frankie,

It was with great pleasure that I learned of your appointment as Managing Director to the Huawei Corporation. I'm cheerful for you since it's a very great company and you are so able and enthusiastic. I believe you will achieve great success in your future career. I would like to express my hearty congratulations to you.

Yours sincerely,

Jack

亲爱的弗兰克：

听到你被华为公司录取为总经理的消息我感到很高兴，华为是一个很不错的公司，而你又热情能干，我相信你在以后的工作中会取得不错的成绩。我向你表达我最真挚的祝贺。

杰克 谨上

邮件回复 *Reply*

Dear Jack,

Thank you for you congratulations. I have never expected to get the offer; you see, there are more than ten qualified candidates applying for the position. I think it was my sincerity that persuaded them. I will work hard to achieve good performance in the post.

Yours sincerely,

Frankie

亲爱的杰克：

感谢你的祝贺。我没有想到他们会给我提供该职位；要知道，有十几个有资历的应征者同时应聘该职位。我想是我的真诚打动了他们吧。我会努力工作争取取得好的成绩。

弗兰克 敬上

范例 10 | 祝贺公司盈利

Dear Cart,

I am writing to congratulate your achieving the total sales of 52,000 units in the third quarter. This significant achievement brings us endless satisfaction and confidence regarding the future. The result also demonstrates your high position in the market.

Yours sincerely,

Sally

亲爱的卡特：

我写信是想向你表达我最热烈的祝贺，祝贺在第三季度贵店销售总量达到了52000台！令我们充满了喜悦和对未来的信心，这个结果也表明贵公司受到市场的高度评价。

赛里 谨上

邮件回复 *Reply*

Dear Sally,

Thank you for your congratulations. This achievement would not have been possible without the outstanding performance of distributors like you.

We are determined to make next season an even bigger one for us all and would like to again ask for your continuing support and cooperation.

Yours sincerely,

Cart

亲爱的赛里：

感谢您的祝贺。这一成绩没有像您一样的分销商的优良表现是不可能的。

我们决心下一季度取得更大的成绩，我们再次请求您的继续支持和合作。

卡特 敬上

范例 11 | 祝贺工作表现

Dear Caroline,

In recognition of your excellent performance in the large project in the first half of the year, the company decided to reward you with ￥15,000 bonus. Besides, your name will be added to the billboard in the lobby next week that acknowledges the Best Employees of the Month.

Your dedication and initiative have made great contribution to the company. Thank you for your splendid contribution.

Congratulations!

Yours sincerely,

Robort

亲爱的卡洛琳：

鉴于你在上半年大项目上突出的表现，公司决定给予15000元的奖金作为奖励。另外，你的名字将作为本月最佳员工于下个星期贴在大厅的公告板上。你的敬业和积极性为公司做出了许多贡献。感谢你的努力。

祝贺你！

罗伯特 谨上

邮件回复 *Reply*

Dear Robert,

What a fantastic surprise I learnt from your mail! I greatly appreciate the bonus. It's always nice to be recognized when you made a little achievement.

I enjoy working with the team here and look forward to more fun ahead!

Yours sincerely,

Caroline

亲爱的罗伯特：

你的邮件带来的是一个多么好的消息啊！非常感谢所提供的奖金。每当你取得一点小成绩的时候就得到认可，这是一件多么美好的事啊！

我非常喜欢在这样一个团队工作，并且期待更多的乐趣。

卡洛琳 敬上

范例 12 | 祝贺员工结婚

Dear Max,

Congratulations on your marriage to Lily.

She's a wonderful girl in every way; you two are a perfect match. I congratulate you for your making a loving pair.

Best wishes for you both. I wish you and your bride the best of luck, and ever-increasing happiness as the years go by.

Yours sincerely,

Jim

亲爱的麦克斯：

祝贺你和莉莉喜结连理。

莉莉是一个各方面都非常好的女孩，你们俩简直是天生一对。我祝你们有情人终成眷属。

请接受我最美好的祝福，我希望你和新娘能行大运，愿你们幸福与年俱增。

杰米 谨上

邮件回复 *Reply*

Dear Jim,

Thank you for your email. We are very happy and feel that we are the luckiest couple in the world. Certainly, it makes us even happier to get your greetings and wishes.

Thank you again.

Yours sincerely,

Max

亲爱的吉姆：

感谢您发的邮件。我们也很高兴，觉得自己是世界上最幸福的一对儿。当然，能够得到您的恭贺和祝福令我们感到更加幸福。

再次感谢。

马克斯 敬上

范例 13 | 祝福朋友结婚

Dear Rita,

What big news! You will be married to Mr. Li next Sunday. Let me offer my warmest congratulations on this happy occasion.

My husband joins me to express our most sincere wishes to you and hope that you have a long, happy and prosperous life together. As a small token of our good wishes, we take pleasure in sending you a small present which will arrive later. At the same time I wish you have a pleasant journey of honeymoon.

May last happiness and joy be yours forever.

Yours sincerely,

Jenny

亲爱的瑞塔：

这真是天大的好消息。你下周日就要和李先生结婚了！在这幸福的时刻，请接受我最温暖的祝福！

我先生和我一起向你表示最诚挚的祝福，祝愿你们美满幸福，相伴到老。我们很高兴寄给了你一个小礼物，聊表心意，稍后即到。同时祝你们蜜月旅行愉快。

愿幸福快乐永远伴随你！

珍妮 谨上

邮件回复 *Reply*

Dear Jenny,

I am sorry to hear that you can't attend our wedding because of business. But it does not matter. I am pleased when I received your present. We don't know how to solve many things about our wedding, I will learn from you. Can you give us some suggestions about how to spend our honeymoon? I hope you and your husband have a good day and work successfully.

Wish you all the best!

Yours sincerely,

Rita

亲爱的珍妮：

很遗憾你们因为有事不能接受我们的邀请来参加我们的婚礼。不过，没有关系。收到你们诚挚的祝福，我已经很开心了。有关婚礼的事我们还有很多不懂，希望到时候能够请教你。婚礼以后，到什么地方度蜜月也希望你多提出一些意见。祝你和你先生生活美满，工作顺利。

祝好！

瑞塔 谨上

范例 14 | 祝贺生子

Dear Mary,

It really takes a long time to have little Jack come to the earth at last. It has been such a long process that is hard for you. I know you have been expecting the wonderful moment. But all that is over now, and the three of your family can live new life happily.

From what I hear, this is definitely an adoption of heaven. I know that Jack will bring a great deal of happiness and surprise to your new life.

Yours sincerely,

Lisa

亲爱的玛丽：

经过漫长的等待，小杰克终于降生了。而且我知道这对你来说是一个辛苦，但充满期待的过程。你一直在期待着这一伟大时刻。但是现在那些都结束了，你们一家三口可以一起开始你们的新生活了。

据我听说，这绝对是上苍对你们的恩赐。我知道杰克会给你们夫妻俩带来无限的幸福和惊喜。

丽萨 谨上

邮件回复 *Reply*

Dear Lisa,

I am very happy to receive your blessing. I still immerse myself in the happiness.

God gives me such a beautiful baby, who makes me proud. From now on, I have to take care of one more person. I will care about him with heart and soul. And let him know that there are so many aunts and uncles loving him.

Yours sincerely,

Mary

亲爱的丽萨：

收到你的祝福我很开心，谢谢你。现在我还沉浸在幸福中。

感谢上天赐予我这样一个漂亮的宝贝，我为他骄傲，从此我的生命中多了一个守护的人，我会用全部的爱去关怀他，让他知道有这么多的叔叔阿姨都爱着他。

玛丽 谨上

范例 15 | 祝贺朋友病愈

Dear Margret,

I am very glad to hear that you have recovered from your illness. We were all very worried about you. And now with your relatives and friends' nurturing and warm caring, your disease is recovering. And those who know you are very glad that you are now recovering. You are a brave man. I am proud to be your friend. I hope that you will soon be completely healthy.

Yours faithfully,

Jessie

亲爱的玛格丽特：

我非常高兴得知你的病情有所好转，之前我们所有人都很担心你。而现在在你的亲戚、朋友的悉心照料和温暖关怀下，你的病正在康复之中，所有认识你的人听到这一消息都很高兴。你是个勇敢的人，我为是你的朋友而感到自豪。希望不久之后你能完全好起来。

杰西 谨上

邮件回复 *Reply*

Dear Jessie,

Thanks for your sympathy with full of encouraging. I am now taking time out to recover. I believe that I would be discharge shortly afterward, and can catch you soon. I miss you so much during this period. Thanks for the encouragement and support. I'm more confident now. I promise that you will see a healthy me.

Yours sincerely,

Margret

亲爱的杰西：

感谢你的慰问与充满鼓励的来信，我现在正在恢复中，我相信再过不久我就可以出院，可以见到你们，这段时间我非常想念你们，想到大家对我的鼓舞与支持，就有了战胜病魔的更多信心，我保证你一定会看到一个健康活泼的我。

玛格丽特 谨上

范例 16 | 祝福朋友家人康复

Dear Mrs. Johnson,

I heard your husband, Mr. John, has been recovered. We are happy for you. We wish to offer you our heartfelt congratulations on the convalescence of your husband. And we hope that he will speedily resume his good health as usual. I believe your husband's recovery cannot come true without your meticulous care.

Yours sincerely,

Ellen

尊敬的约翰逊夫人：

听说您丈夫约翰逊先生已经痊愈，我们都替您感到高兴，并对您致以最诚挚的祝福，祝福您的丈夫逐渐康复。并且我们希望他能很快健康如昔。相信您先生的痊愈和您无微不至的照料是分不开的。

埃伦 谨上

邮件回复 *Reply*

Dear Ellen,

Thank your for your wishes during the period of my husband's staying in hospital. He has recovered now. But the doctor said that he should stay at home for several days. Thank you for your caring. He will go back to work soon. How are you now? Please do more exercise everyday.

Wish you healthy!

Yours sincerely,

Mrs. Johnson

亲爱的埃伦：

谢谢你在我丈夫生病期间送来的祝福。我丈夫现在已经康复了。不过，医生说他还需要在家休养一段时间。谢谢你的关心，他很快会回去工作的。你最近身体可好？要记得每天多锻炼身体！

祝身体健康！

约翰逊夫人 谨上

范例 17 | 恭贺梦想成真

Dear Jone,

We are so excited that you have expanded your company successfully. We all know that you have the intention to expand the size of company, aiming at making greater achievement in business. Few firms can do what you have achieved in such a short period of time. In my perspective, your strong leadership and the efforts of all the staff attribute to your magnificent success.

Please accept our genuine congratulations and best wishes for your lasting success.

Yours sincerely,

Jack

亲爱的约恩：

得知贵公司扩大规模的消息，我们很振奋。我们知道一直以来你都致力于扩大公司规模，在事业上取得更大的成就。向来少有公司在这么短的时间内取得像贵公司这样的成就。在我们眼里。这份巨大的成功归功于你的卓越的领导才能和上下员工的一致努力。

请接受我们最衷心地祝贺，并预祝贵方不断取得成功。

杰克 谨上

邮件回复 *Reply*

Dear Jack,

Thanks for your congratulations. I am also very happy that I, after years' efforts, eventually realize my dreams. My mood is very excited. Of course, I cannot make it without your assistance in business. I hope the cooperation between us can be more enjoyable and we look forward to jointly developing greater business space.

Yours,

Jone

亲爱的杰克：

感谢你的祝贺，我自己也很开心，现在这么多年来的梦想终于得以实现，心情也很激动，当然这一切都离不开你们在事业上的帮助，希望以后与贵公司的合作能更愉快，期待我们共同开发更广阔的事业空间。

约恩 谨上

范例 18 | 祝福结婚纪念

Dear Jane,

You are so lucky to have the privilege to add a tribute congratulatory to twenty-five years of wedded life. On such a sweet occasion, memory draws on the tranquilities and vicissitudes experienced. The thoughts turning from the cares, troubles, and anxieties, review with more cheerful time and felicities of the past, it is so natural for us to see only the brightness but the shadows, even though it is only the "silver wedding" .

With such pleasant memories, my wife and I hope that you can move on through life's journey, and be strewn with flowers of kindness and affection. And we hope that you can see the foreshadowing of a blessed future while looking at the bright, pure surface of the gift accompanying this.

Yours sincerely,

Bart

亲爱的简：

你们很幸运能够拥有为持续25年的婚姻生活庆贺的机会。在这甜蜜时刻，记忆在平静与过往中逐渐浮现出来。从前种种关心、麻烦与懊恼中，伴随着的是更多的快乐和幸福，即使仅是银婚，已经让我们忽略了种种阴霾，只看到眼前的幸福。

有如此愉快的回忆相伴，我和我妻子希望你们能继续享受生命的旅程，并且希望你们一路上都被善良与温情的鲜花簇拥。随之奉上的这光明的、纯洁的礼物，希望可以让你看到未来的幸福前景。

巴特 谨上

读书笔记

邮件回复 *Reply*

Dear Bart,

Thank you for your wishes. Life is full of happiness and sadness. It is not easy for us to be together for such a long time. We will treasure our marriage. People can only become more mature in the marriage. I believe that you have the same experience. What makes us admire is that , though you two just get married, you act like an old couple. I hope you can live with your wife harmoniously, and manage the family together.

Wish you happy!

Yours sincerely,

Jane

亲爱的巴特：

非常感谢你的祝福。生活中充满幸福和悲伤，但我们一路走来的确不容易。我们会更加珍惜我们的婚姻。人只有在婚礼中才能更加成熟。相信你也有很多体会。你和妻子刚结婚不久，但你们之间的恩爱像老夫妻一样，这也让我们很羡慕。希望你也能和妻子在今后更加和睦相处，共同经营家庭。

祝你们幸福！

简 谨上

读书笔记

范例 19 | 祝福演讲成功

Dear Lisa,

Your speech this morning was exactly what we needed to hear about global environmental protection. Each slide was clear and concise, and every point refers to current environmental problem. Furthermore, your handouts of the final conclusion will help us strengthen our surrounding environmental protection.

Yours sincerely,

Eric

亲爱的丽萨：

你今天上午的演讲恰恰是我们需要听到的，关于全球环境保护的问题。每个幻灯片都很清晰而且简明扼要，每一点都谈到了当今环境问题。另外，你最后一段的总结演说更是有助于帮助我们加强周围的环境保护力度。

艾瑞克 谨上

邮件回复 *Reply*

Dear Eric,

Thank you for your listening to my lecture. I prepared this lecture for a long time. I collected a lot of materials in this field. I also consulted some experts in some questions. The environmental problem is more serious than before. The purpose of this lecture is to call for more people to do something for the environment protection. If everyone can do something, the world will be better. I also hope you can drive the friends in your side to protect the environment.

Wish you all the best!

Yours sincerely

Lisa

亲爱的艾瑞克：

非常感谢你能倾听我的演讲。这次演讲是我花了很长时间精心准备，收集了很多的相关资料而成的。在有些方面还咨询了一些专家和学者的意见。因为现在环境问题越来越严重。我这次演讲的目的就是号召更多的人加入到环境保护的行列之中。每个人尽出一份力，世界会变得更加美好。希望你也能够带动身边的朋友来一起保护环境。

祝愿你一切都好！

丽萨 谨上

范例 20 | 祝贺订婚

Dear Aaron,

I have just heard that you will engaged to the woman you love. It's the most joyful news I have heard for a long time. Congratulations and best wishes to you.

I think it is the most wonderful thing in the world. And from now on, you will have a fiancee who will love you and take care of you and be a part of your life. Life will be beautiful and happy with the women you love so much. I wish you can enjoy your life with her.

Allow me to offer my heartiest congratulations on your engagement.

Yours sincerely,

Tom

亲爱的艾伦：

我刚刚听说你和心爱的女人订婚的消息。这是我最近听到的最棒的喜讯。衷心地祝贺并祝福你。

我想这应该是世界上最美好的事情。从现在开始，你将会有个爱你、照顾你的未婚妻。她会成为你生命中的一部分。和你爱的人一起，生活将会是美好和愉快的。我衷心地希望你和她能享受现在的生活。

允许我为你送上最真挚的祝福。

汤姆 谨上

邮件回复 *Reply*

Dear Tom,

Thank you for your blessing. I am very happy to receive the blessing from my best friend.

Lucy and I havc been dating for three years before this day finally comes. I am very happy, very excited. I want to share my joy with you. You have witnessed our love. Thank you for your sincere blessing. We will be together forever.

May you find your lover as soon as possible.

Yours sincerely,

Aaron

亲爱的汤姆：

非常感谢你的来信，谢谢你的祝福。我很高兴能够得到最好朋友的祝福。

我和露西交往了三年，这一天终于来了。我很开心，很激动。我很想和你一起分享这份喜悦。你见证了我们的爱情，谢谢你真挚的祝福。我们将会永不分离。

愿你早日找到自己的另一半。

艾伦 谨上

范例 21 | 祝贺获胜

Dear Aaron,

I am writing to convey my congratulations on your success on the tennis tournament. I am happy that your hard work and genius have been rewarded.

You have prepared for this tournament for a long time, and practiced very hard. I think you deserve it. I am so proud of you. Maybe we should have a dinner together to talk all about this game to share your happiness. And I am looking forward to hearing more good news about your games.

Congratulations and best wishes to you!

Yours sincerely,

Tom

亲爱的艾伦：

祝贺你在网球锦标赛上获得成功。我很高兴你的才能和勤奋得到了回报。

你为了这个比赛准备了相当长的一段时间，练习得非常勤奋。我想这是你应得的。也许我们需要约个时间把酒言欢，好好的谈论这场比赛，分享你的喜悦。我期待听到你比赛更多的好消息。

恭喜你，也祝福你！

汤姆 谨上

邮件回复 *Reply*

Dear Tom,

Thank you for your praise and congratulations. I am also looking forward to meeting you and sharing my experience with you.

Best wishes!

Yours sincerely,

Aaron

亲爱的汤姆：

非常感谢你的肯定和祝贺。我也非常期待和你分享一下我的比赛经历。

祝好！

艾伦 谨上

范例 22 | 祝贺公司周年

Dear Aaron,

Congratulations on the thirty anniversaries of your company. As your friend, I have witnessed the growth of the company, and know that each staff has paid a lot. I really admire your efforts and pay.

Now it is growing rapidly. The scalc of the company is expanding. It is in a good position in this industry. More and more people know more and more about the products. Although there were many crisis and challenges, you had overcome all of them. It's like you child, becoming better under your good caring. I hope you can continue to work hard to gain greater success!

Yours sincerely,

Tom

亲爱的艾伦：

恭喜你的公司建立三十周年。作为你的朋友，我见证了这个公司的成长以及你和每位员工对它的付出。我非常敬佩你们的努力和付出。

现在的它正处于快速成长时期。公司的规模在不断扩大，在这个行业也取得了很好的地位。人们对于产品也越来越熟知。虽然也有过危机和挑战，但是你都克服了。它就像你的孩子，在你精心照顾下，成长的越来越好。希望你们能够继续努力，获得更大的成功！

汤姆 谨上

读书笔记

邮件回复 *Reply*

Dear Tom,

Thank you for your letter. It has been thirty years since I set up the company, and it feels like yesterday. During so many years, I have got a lot of experience and feelings here. I appreciate my employees and my family members. I have got so much support from them. And I also appreciate my dear friends. In this process, you give me a lot of advice and encouragement. I really appreciate your help.

Bless you!

Yours sincerely,

Aaron

亲爱的汤姆：

谢谢你的来信。转眼三十多年过去了，想到当初刚刚建立它的时候，就像是在昨天。经过这么多年，我在这里获得了很多经验和感受。我非常感谢我的员工和家人对我的支持，同样也感谢我亲爱的朋友。在这个过程中你给了我很多建议和鼓励，非常感谢你对我的帮助。

祝福你！

艾伦 谨上

读书笔记

范例 23 | 新年祝福

Dear Catherine,

New Year is coming soon. I am so happy to celebrate the holiday with you. Thank you for always helping me. Wish the New Year will bring you health and happiness. And wish you all dreams come true.

Happy New Year!

Yours sincerely,

Denise

亲爱的凯瑟琳：

转眼新的一年到了。在这个美好的日子里，能与你一起欢庆，我很高兴。谢谢你一直以来对我的帮助。祝你新的一年，梦想成真，身体健康，生活愉快！

新年快乐！

丹尼斯 谨上

邮件回复 *Reply*

Dear Denise,

Happy New Year to you too! I am happy to receive your letter. And I also wish you happy all the time.

Yours sincerely,

Catherine

亲爱的丹尼斯：

也祝你新年快乐！我很高兴收到你的来信。也希望你能永远开心。

凯瑟琳 谨上

读书笔记

范例 24 | 圣诞祝福

Dear Catherine,

Here comes the Christmas Day. And Merry Christmas! Every year we will go back to our hometown and celebrate the holiday with friends, families and you! It is a wonderful thing to have a good time with all of you. I wish you can all have a good life and healthy body.

Yours sincerely,

Denise

亲爱的凯瑟琳：

圣诞节就要来了。圣诞快乐！每年我们都从不同地方回到我们的家乡与我们的朋友、亲人，还有你一起庆祝这个美好的节日。能够和你们一起度过这个节日真的很棒。希望你们都有美好的生活，健康的身体。

丹尼斯 谨上

邮件回复 *Reply*

Dear Denise,

Merry Christmas to my friend! I am glad to hear from you. I am also very happy to have the good time with you. And I also hope you can have a better life too.

Yours sincerely,

Catherine

亲爱的丹尼斯：

亲爱的朋友，圣诞快乐！我很高兴你能那么说。我也很高兴能和你一起度过这个美好的时刻。我也祝你有更好的生活。

凯瑟琳 谨上

读书笔记

范例 25 | 主要节日词汇一览表

1月1日　元旦（New Year's Day）
2月14日　情人节（Valentine's Day）
3月8日　国际妇女节（International Women' Day）
3月12日　中国植树节（China Arbor Day）
3月14日　白色情人节（White Day）
4月1日　愚人节（April Fools' Day）
4月5日　清明节（Tomb-sweeping Day）
5月1日　国际劳动节（International Labour Day）
5月4日　中国青年节（Chinese Youth Day）
5月8日　世界红十字日（World Red-Cross Day）
5月12日　国际护士节（International Nurse Day）
5月15日　国际家庭日（International Family Day）
5月17日　世界电信日（World Telecommunications Day）
5月20日　全国学生营养日（National Students' Nutrition Day）
5月22日　国际生物多样性日（International Biodiversity Day）
5月31日　世界无烟日（World No Tabacco Day）
6月1日　国际儿童节（International Children's Day）
6月5日　世界环境日（International Environment Day）
6月6日　全国爱眼日（National Eye-care Day）
6月17日　世界防治荒漠化和干旱日（World Day to Combat Desertification）
6月23日　国际奥林匹克日（International Olympic Day）
6月25日　全国土地日（National Land Day）
6月26日　国际禁毒日（International Day Against Drug Abuse and Illicit Trafficking）
7月1日　国际建筑日（International Architecture Day）
7月7日　中国人民抗日战争纪念日（Chinese People's Anti-Japanese War Anniversary）
7月11日　世界人口日（World Population Day）
8月1日　中国人民解放军建军节（Army Day）
8月12日　国际青年节（International Youth Day）
9月8日　国际扫盲日（International Literacy Day）

9月10日　中国教师节（Teacher's Day）
9月16日　中国脑健康日（Chinese Brain Health Day）
9月20日　全国爱牙日（National Love Teeth Day）
9月21日　世界停火日（World Cease-fire Day）
9月27日　世界旅游日（World Tourism Day）
10月1日　中华人民共和国国庆节（National Day）
10月1日　国际音乐日（International Music Day）
10月1日　国际老年人日（International Day of Older Persons）
10月4日　世界动物日（World Animal Day）
10月5日　世界教师日（World Teachers' Day）（联合国教科文组织确立）
10月8日　全国高血压日（National High Blood Pressure Day）
10月9日　世界邮政日（World Post Day）
10月10日　世界精神卫生日（World Mental Health Day）
10月14日　世界标准日（World Standards Day）
10月15日　国际盲人节（International Day of the Blind）
10月15日　世界农村妇女日（World Rural Women's Day）
10月16日　世界粮食日（World Food Day）
10月17日　国际消除贫困日（International Day for the Eradication of Poverty）
10月24日　联合国日（United Nations Day）
10月24日　世界发展新闻日（World Development Information Day）
10月28日　中国男性健康日（Chinese Men's Health Day）
10月31日　万圣节（Halloween）
11月8日　中国记者节（Journalists' Day）
11月9日　消防宣传日（Fire Awareness Day）
11月14日　世界糖尿病日（World Diabetes Day）
11月17日　国际大学生节（International College Students' Day）
11月25日　国际消除对妇女的暴力日
（International Day for the Elimination of Violence against Women）
12月1日　世界艾滋病日（World AIDS Day）
12月3日　世界残疾人日（World Disabled Day）
12月4日　全国法制宣传日（National Legal Publicity Day）
12月9日　世界足球日（World Football Day）

12月25日　圣诞节（Christmas Day）

1月最后一个星期日　国际麻风节（International Leprosy Day）

3月最后一个完整周的星期一　中小学生安全教育日
（Primary and Middle School Students Safety Education Day）

春分月圆后的第一个星期日　复活节（Easter Day）
（有可能是3月22日~4月25日的任一天）

5月第二个星期日　母亲节（Mother's Day）

5月的第三个星期二　国际牛奶日（International Milk Day）

5月第三个星期日　全国助残日（National Day of Assisting Disabled Persons）

6月第三个星期日　父亲节（Father's Day）

9月第21日　国际和平日（International Peace Day）

9月第三个星期六　全国国防教育日（National Defense Education Day）

9月第四个星期日　国际聋人节（International Day of the Deaf）

10月的第一个星期一　世界住房日（World Habitat Day）

10月的第二个星期一　加拿大感恩节（Thanksgiving Day）

10月第二个星期三　国际减轻自然灾害日
（International Day for Natural Disaster Reduction）

10月第二个星期四　世界爱眼日（World Sight Day）

11月最后一个星期四　美国感恩节（Thanksgiving Day）

农历节日

农历正月初一　春节（the Spring Festival）

农历正月十五　元宵节（Lantern Festival）

农历五月初五　端午节（the Dragon-Boat Festival）

农历七月初七　乞巧节（中国情人节）（Double-Seventh Day）

农历八月十五　中秋节（the Mid-Autumn Festival）

农历九月初九　重阳节（the Double Ninth Festival）

农历腊月初八　腊八节（the Laba Rice Porridge Festival）

Unit 9 吊唁篇

（1）如何写

a）首先写明自己对收到的信息表示震惊、遗憾；

b）说明失去某人是对方的极大的损失，安慰对方；赞扬逝世之人的品德与事迹；表达如果对方需要，自己愿意尽其所能给予帮助；

c）给予对方最深切的慰问。

（2）实用例句

a）I heard you had lost... This is such a dreadful shock; and I just want to tell you that I am so sorry to hear this news.

我听说……去世了，这真是个可怕的消息。我只想告诉你听到这个消息我很难过。

b）I am sorry for your losing of your lover.

我很难过你失去了你的爱人。

c）We will miss him forever.

我们将会永远怀念他。

d）But the good memories will comfort you.

但是回忆将会陪伴着你，安慰你。

e）If you need help, please let me know, and I will try my best...

如果你需要帮助，请告诉我，我会竭尽所能……

f）The sudden passing of him was a great shock to me.

他的突然过世让我很震惊。

g）I hope you can live on.

我希望你可以继续好好地活着。

h）Please accept my sincere condolence.

请接受我真挚的吊唁。

i）You have my heartfelt sympathy.

送上我发自内心的同情。

范例 1 | 对合作伙伴的吊唁

Dear Mrs. Bart,

I was shocked to know Mr. Bart had passed away and I am writing now to express my deep sympathy.

I know Mr. Bart for many years and always thought him as a personal friend. He is wise, kind and honest. It is really a pleasure of doing business together with him. I will miss him forever.

Please accept my deepest sympathy and bring my best wishes to your family.

Yours sincerely,

Nelly

亲爱的巴特夫人：

得知巴特先生去世的消息后，我深感表悲痛，现向您表达我们深切的哀悼之情。

我认识巴特先生许多年了，把他当作一个亲切的朋友看待。他是一个聪明、善良、正直的人，和他合作生意是一件很愉快的事。我会永久想念他。

请接受我们最深的悼念和对你的家庭最诚挚的祝福。

内莉 谨上

邮件回复 *Reply*

Dear Nelly,

Your mail is a great solace for me. God is cruel in such an act. I find it difficult to spend my days without my husband. My life seems to be of no value.

Either way, I am grateful to you for your smoothening mail.

With thanks.

Yours sincerely,

Lily Bart

亲爱的内莉：

你的邮件给了我很大的安慰。上帝真是太残忍了。没有我丈夫的日子实在是太难过了。我的生活似乎都没有意义了。

不管怎样，我非常感谢您的安慰。

谢谢！

莉莉 · 巴特 敬上

范例 2 | 代表公司吊唁

Dear Mrs. Beck,

On behalf of my colleagues and myself, I am writing to you to express our most sincere sympathy on this sad occasion when Mr. Beck passed away.

Mr. Beck was a commercial big shot in the business circles. We respect him very much as he was a man of wisdom and credit.

Please accept our deepest sympathy and show our sympathy to your family.

Yours sincerely,

CW Corporation

亲爱的贝克夫人：

听闻贵公司的董事长贝克先生去世的消息，谨代表我和我的同事，在这个沉痛的时候，写信向你表达我最真诚的悼念。

贝克先生是商界的大亨。我们十分尊敬他，他是一个非常智慧和有声望的人。

请接受我在此向您及您的家人最深切的同情。

CW公司 敬上

邮件回复 *Reply*

Dear staff,

Thank you for your kind letter and your time to attend my husband's funeral service.

I felt quite happy to know that my husband was loved, respected and counted on by so many people. And I am rather proud that he enjoyed and devoted his life to working for the prosperity of the firm with which he was related.

Thank you all.

Yours sincerely,

Mona Beck

尊敬的诸位：

感谢大家的问候，并参加我丈夫的丧礼。

看到我的丈夫为那么多人所喜爱、尊敬和重视，这使我感到特别欣慰。我的丈夫为他的公司奉献了毕生，并且乐在其中，我感到十分骄傲。

感谢大家。

莫纳·贝克 谨上

范例 3 | 回复吊唁

Dear Mr. Huang,

Your warm thoughts and expression of condolence are deeply appreciated. Nothing can console me more than the sincere sympathy of one of my beloved husband's friends.

A large number of his colleagues and friends paid him final tribute at the funeral service held on April 5. It made me feel very happy and honored to know that my husband was loved, respected and counted on by so many people.

I would like to extend to you my sincerest thanks for your longstanding friendship and the invaluable support you afforded my husband.

Yours sincerely,

Maria Black

尊敬的黄先生：

十分感谢您善意的问候。来自我丈夫的朋友真诚的同情最能安慰我的痛苦。

4月5日举行的追悼会上，他的许多同事和朋友都赶来缅怀。看到我的丈夫为那么多人所喜爱、尊敬和重视，这使我感到特别欣慰和骄傲。

对您长期以来给予我丈夫的友谊和帮助我表示最诚挚的谢意。

玛利亚 · 布莱克 谨上

邮件回复 *Reply*

Dear Mrs. Black,

We appreciate your great manner on this sad occasion. And we wish you can soon get out of the hurt. If you need any help, please feel free to tell us.

Yours sincerely,

Huang Zhong

尊敬的布莱克夫人：

我们非常欣赏您在这一悲痛时刻所保有的良好风范。我们希望您能尽快走出悲痛的阴影。如果您需要帮助，请不吝赐知。

黄忠 敬上

范例 4 | 讣文

Feb. 14, 2019

Black Lively, chief editor of *Heart-To-Heart Talk*, died at 81.

He was born in 1930, graduated from Michigan University in 1953, entered in *Heart-To-Heart Talk* in 1954.

He was a soft-spoken and obsessive man. He was always very dutiful and strict with his work and he's pretty glad to offer help and support to his colleagues. The dedication made by him contributed a lot to *Heart-To-Heart Talk*, his colleagues respect him so much. In the final days of his life, he showed his optimism and strong will.

We are extremely sorry for his death and express our sincerest bless for him and his family.

布莱克·来弗利，《知心话》杂志主编，于2019年2月14日去世，享年81岁。

布莱克先生出生于1930年，于1953年从密歇根大学毕业，1954年进入《知心话》杂志。

他是一个善言有魅力的人，他一直都尽职尽责，严于律己，他总是乐于助人，帮助同事。他对杂志贡献很多，同事们都十分尊敬他。在他最后的时光里，他展现给我们的是他乐观与坚强的形象。

我们对他的去世感到深深的遗憾，同时也真心祝福他和他的家庭。

读书笔记

范例 5 | 吊唁亲人逝世

Dear Robin,

I was grieved to hear of Maureen's passing away. Please accept my deepest sympathies to you and your family.

Maureen is my favorite sister. I will always remember her active outlook on life, her generous nature, and warm feelings towards anyone who required her help. But above all, I shall mostly miss her for her wonderful sense of responsibility which had always made our days safe and sound.

I again feel deeply sorrowful at the news of Maureen's passing. My family and I send our love and our assurance of devoted friendship now. Should you need any help with the arrangements or anything else I can do, please inform me.

Yours truly,

Daisy

亲爱的罗宾：

听到莫林的丧讯我很伤心。请接受我在此向你及你的家人表示我最深切的同情。

莫林是我最喜欢的姐姐。我将永远记得她对待生活积极乐观的态度，还有她慨然大方的性格及对每一个向她寻求帮助的人都热情相待的精神。不仅如此，我更怀念她极强的责任感，使我们天天生活得安全、舒心。

我再次对莫林的去世表示深深的哀悼。我的家人及我个人向你们表示最真诚的关爱并会同你们保持永远忠实的友谊。如果你们在后事安排上需要帮助或者其他我能帮上忙的，请告诉我。

黛西 谨上

邮件回复 *Reply*

Dear Daisy,

Thank you very much for your help and condolences during the funeral. During the past few months we have sunk in mourning. Your enlightment makes us relieve from the sadness. Thank you for your help. We believe that Maureen has not left, and she is always here with us. Thanks again for your charity.

Yours,

Robin

亲爱的黛西：

非常感谢你在我们家丧事期间所给予的帮助与慰问。这几个月来我们一直沉浸在悲痛之中，但是在你的耐心开导下，我们感到非常宽慰，多谢你的帮助。我们相信莫林并未离去，她一直就守候在我们身边。再次感谢你的善举。

罗宾 谨上

范例 6 | 吊唁朋友

Dear Robin,

I was grieved to hear of Maureen's passing away. Please accept my deepest sympathies to you and your family.

Maureen was a good friend to me while we shared the same apartment at Peking University. What impressed me most is her active attitude towards life, her generous nature, and warm feelings towards those who required her help. But above all, I shall mostly miss her for her wonderful sense of responsibility which had always made our days safe and sound.

I again feel deeply sorrowful at the news of Maureen's passing. My family and I send our love and our assurance of devoted friendship now. Should you need any help with the arrangements or anything else I can do, please inform me.

Yours truly,

Daisy

亲爱的罗宾：

听到莫林的丧讯我很伤心。请接受我在此向你及你的家人表示我最深切的同情。

莫林是我在北京大学时同宿舍的好朋友。我将永远记得她对待生活积极乐观的态度，还有她慨然大方的性格及对每一个向她寻求帮助的人都热情相待的精神。不仅如此，我更怀念她极强的责任感，使我们天天生活得安全、舒心。

我再次对莫林的去世表示深深的哀悼。我的家人及我个人向你们表示最真诚的关爱并会同你们保持永远忠实的友谊。如果你们在后事安排上需要帮助或者其他我能帮上忙的，请告诉我。

黛西 谨上

邮件回复 Reply

Dear Daisy,

Thank you for your concern. I heard from Maureen that you were her best friend in the university. You had given a lot of help to her in both life and study. Thank you very much. She often said she was very happy to be friends with you. Her most regret was that she didn't graduate from the university. She hoped you can work hard to complete her wish.

Wish you good health!

Yours sincerely,

Robin

亲爱的黛西：

谢谢你的关心。听莫林说你是她在学校最好的朋友。你在学习和生活中给了她很大的帮助。在此表示感谢。她说她很高兴能和你成为朋友。她最大的遗憾就是没有读完大学。希望你能好好学习，完成莫林的心愿。

祝你身体健康！

罗宾 谨上

读书笔记

Unit 10 咨询篇

（1）如何写

a）咨询信是写信人就自己不熟悉和不理解的事情或问题，向有关部门或专家请求解答时所使用的一种专用书信；

b）咨询信通常由标题、称呼、正文、结尾、落款等几个部分组成；

c）咨询信的内容主要是将自己的问题如实地向对方提出来，要把起因、状况、结果、需要对方回答的问题具体清楚地写出来，以便对方知道你所询问的问题，正确回答你的问题。

（2）实用例句

a）I really appreciate it if you could provide me some essential information.

如果你们可以向我提供一些有用的信息，我将不胜感激。

b）We would like to know further information about the prices of the goods.

我们希望更多地了解有关产品价格的信息。

c）I am interested in your project, but I feel confused in some aspects.

我对你的项目很感兴趣，但在几个方面我有疑问。

d）Can you send some pictures of the machine to our mail address?

你们可以发一些这台机器的图片到我们邮箱吗？

e）How long will you deliver the goods to us?

你们多久能把货物交给我们？

f）And is there any condition for agreement, such as...?

在协议上还有条件吗？例如……

g）And as usual, how long would such vegetables be kept in fresh?

通常，这样的蔬菜能保鲜多久？

h）Could you please give me all samples to let me choose my favorite one?

你能把所有的样品给我，让我选择我最中意的吗？

范例 1 | 询问公司信息

Dear Mr. Smith,

From your advertisement in the March 28, issue of *Foreign Trade*, we understand that your company specializes in the export of various light industrial products and that you are making effort to extend overseas trade. We are contacting you with a view to introducing some of your products into our market. Therefore, we need more detailed information about your business.

We have been in the import and export business for over 30 years. It appears that demand for light industrial products is now increasing and we believe that your corporation has the ability to do considerable business in this area.

We would appreciate it very much if you could send us your latest catalogues for the items, as well as price lists for the various lines and your terms and conditions of sales.

We look forward to your early reply.

Yours sincerely,

Wang Lin

尊敬的史密斯先生：

我们从3月13号出版的《对外贸易》杂志上刊登的广告上获悉贵公司专营各种轻工业产品的出口业务，并力求扩展海外市场。我们为此联系贵公司，希望能引进你们的产品。因此，我们需要对你们公司做进一步了解。

我们公司经营进出口业务已达30多年。目前，我地对轻工业产品的需求不断增加，相信贵公司在我地的业务将非常可观。

请寄给我方你们关于你们公司产品的最新目录，价目表，并告知相关的销售条款。我们将不胜感激。

盼复

王林 敬上

邮件回复 *Reply*

Dear Mr. Wang,

We thank you for your e-mail of May 3rd, and we are glad to learn that you wish to know more about our company.

In compliance with your request, we are sending you a catalogue, together with a range of pamphlets.

If you have additional questions after reading our introduction, please call our company's sales representative who would be happy to discuss it with you. A list of regional offices and telephone numbers will be enclosed.

We appreciate your interest in our corporation.

Yours truly,

John Smith

尊敬的王先生:

感谢您5月3日的电邮，欣闻您想对我们公司做进一步了解。

应你方请求，我方已将一份目录及公司产品图片寄予你方.

如果您阅读了我们公司的简介后还有其他问题，请致电您所在区域的我公司的地区办事处。随函附上一份地区办事处和电话号码表。

感谢您对我们公司的兴趣。

约翰 · 史密斯 谨上

读书笔记

范例 2 | 询问银行业务

Dear Sir or Madam:

The approaching of the Spring Festival is likely to lead to a considerable increase in my turnover. But since my stocks are exceedingly low and I am unable to obtain long-term credit from the wholesalers. Therefore, we are planning to apply for an overdraft of ￥50,000 from your bank.

And drawings would be spread over a period of one month, ending by March 29, 2011.

I would point out that credit is withheld from me merely because my business has not been established many years, thus making me unable to provide the necessary references, but I should allow you to access to my books of account, from which you could satisfy yourself of the promptitude with my payments are usually made.

We shall be grateful if you could advice us on the following:

application procedure

interest rate

all other fees charged

We look forward to your early reply.

Yours sincerely,

James

敬启者：

由于春节即将来临，我预想我公司产品销售量将大幅上升。但我目前存货甚为不足，而且也不能从批发商取得长期的赊账。因此，我方希望贵银行能预支我方5万元。

所开支票将以1个月为期，到2011年3月29日截止。

我想指出的是我之所以不能得到批发商的信用，是因为从事此行业未久，致使我无法提供必需的证明人，但是，我可允许贵行查核账目。您可发现我方通常都是及时付款的。

如果您能为我们提供以下资料，将不胜感激：

申请程序

利率

其他相关手续费

期待您的早日回复。

詹姆斯 谨上

邮件回复 *Reply*

Dear James,

With regard to your letter of Jan. 3rd, we regret to state that we are unable to comply with your request in its present form. If you could provide a guarantor, or if this is not possible, to deposit with us some collateral security such as share certificates.

We would point out that these precautions are a general practice, not intended to have any personal significance.

We look forward to working with you in the future if possible.

Yours faithfully,

Jack Smith

尊敬的詹姆斯：

您1月3号来函收悉，很抱歉我们现在尚不能遵照您请求的方式行事。如果您能提供担保人，或提供入股份证件等附带担保品交由我方保存的话，我方是愿意考虑此项贷款的。

我们想指出的是此项谨慎举措为一般性手续，并无针对个人的用意。

如有可能，我们期待在将来合作的机会。

杰克·史密斯 敬上

读书笔记

范例 3 | 询问产品信息

Dear Sir or Madam,

Recently, we are interested in importing cotton bed-sheets and pillowcases. Mr. Frank Norris of the ABC Company advises us that your company is supplying these items.

We would like you to send us details of your various ranges, including sizes, colors and also samples of the different qualities of material used, and prices quoted should include insurance and freight to Wuhan.

We are large dealers in Mainland China and believe there is a promising market in our area for your goods.

Besides, please let me know how much your company can supply from stock and your earliest date of delivery. In addition, I would like to know if your company is prepared to grant a 10% discount.

Yours truly,

William

敬启者：

目前，我们公司需要引进棉床单和枕套。ABC公司的法兰克·诺里斯先生告诉我们贵公司生产我们所需要的产品。

请告诉我方有关你方产品型号和颜色的详细信息，并附上不同材质的样品。你方报价应包括运输至武汉的保险费及运费。

我们是中国大陆的大型运营商，我们相信你方产品会在这里拥有广阔的市场前景。

此外，请告诉我方贵公司现货的数量和最快的送货日期。并且，我希望知道贵公司是否同意给予10%的折扣。

威廉姆 谨上

读书笔记

邮件回复 *Reply*

Dear Mr. William,

Thank you for your inquiry for additional information on the bed-sheets and pillowcases, which we have been producing since 1995.

Our company has an excellent reputation for high-quality products, durability and service. Our products are designed and manufactured in China.

I have enclosed a special folder on the bed-sheets and pillowcases and a catalog that describes different sizes and colors of the bed-sheets and pillowcases. Also, we invite your attention to our other products such as tablecloth and table napkins, details of which you will find in the catalogue.

We look forward to receiving your first order.

Yours truly,

Li Qing

尊敬的威廉姆先生：

感谢您来函询问棉床单和枕套的相关信息。我方从1995年起就从事该产品的生产。

我方以生产优质产品，耐用性强，服务好在业内享有盛誉。我们的产品在中国设计和制造。

附件是一份专用手册和有关于产品种类的目录。同时，您也可以看一下我公司其他产品。如桌布和餐巾，详见目录。

我们非常期待接到与您的第一份订单。

李清 谨上

读书笔记

范例 4 | 询问交易条件

Dear Mr. Theo,

We are in receipt of your letter of July 3. After reading through your catalog and examining the sample, we find that the quality of the goods is satisfactory. They really impressed us. But before placing an order with you, we would like to inquire the detailed information for this trading.

Will you please offer us a quantity discount in addition to a 10% trade discount off the net list prices? It could be appreciated if you could state your definite prices, detailed specifications, earliest delivery date, terms of payment. If you can assure us of workable prices, excellent quality and prompt delivery, we shall be able to deal in these goods on a substantial scale.

As for our credit standing, please refer to Bank of China, Guangzhou branch.

Your immediate reply would be appreciated.

Yours faithfully,

Fred

尊敬的西奥先生：

收到您于6月3号的来信，我方在阅读了贵公司的产品目录及检查了样品之后，发现产品质量非常令人满意，这给我们留下了深刻的印象。在下订单之前，我方想进一步了解这次交易的详细信息。

除了给我们打个9折，如果我们订购大量产品的话能否再打个折。若你方能详说价格，具体规格，交货日期和付款方式，我方将不胜感激。若您能保证一个可行的价格，上乘的质量和及时的交货，我们将大规模订购该类产品。

中国银行广州分行将为我们提供信誉保证。

期待您的早日答复。

佛瑞德 谨上

邮件回复 *Reply*

Dear Fred,

We have received your letter of March 10th, 2010 inquiring about the trade terms. In response, we enclose our latest price list. We are pleased to quote as follows,

Men's style at US$20 per set

Women's style at US$25 per set

Remarks:

All prices CIF Singapore

Payment by irrevocable L/C at sight

Delivery, within 30 days after receipt of L/C

We look forward to receiving your order. If you have any queries, please do not hesitate to let us know.

Yours sincerely,

Theo

尊敬的佛瑞德先生：

我方已收到你方于3月10号询问交易条件的来信。我们已随函附上我们最新的价目表。

我们的报价如下：

男款每套20美元

女款每套25美元

注意：

均是新加坡到岸价

见不可撤销信用证即付款

收到信用证的30天内交货

我方期待收到你方的订单。如还有疑问，请告诉我方。

西奥 谨上

读书笔记

范例 5 | 询问库存状况

Dear Mr. Bert,

We are pleased to tell you that the computer Acer B-123 sells well in our area. Because of its high configuration and favorable price, they enjoy an increasing popularity among our customers.

Therefore we hope to order more sets. Please confirm your inventory to see if you have twenty more for another delivery.

We all speak highly of your company in last cooperation, including the high quality of products and services. We believe that you won't let us down this time.

If you wish to make inquires concerning our financial status, you may refer to the Bank of Communications.

Looking forward to your early reply.

Yours sincerely,

Tom

尊敬的伯特先生：

贵公司宏基B-123型电脑在我地非常畅销。由于高配置和价格优势，它受到越来越多的客户的喜爱。

因此我方决定加大订货量，麻烦您确认一下该型号是否还有库存，我们需要额外引进20台。

上次的合作，让我方对贵公司大加赞赏。包括你们提供的优质产品和服务。我方相信这次贵公司也不会让我们失望的。

如果您想咨询我们的财务状况，可咨询交通银行。

期待您的早日回复。

汤姆 谨上

读书笔记

邮件回复 Reply

Dear Tom,

We are delighted to receive your letter of November 18 asking whether we can supply you with more Acer B-123. However, we regret to tell you that the goods are not available in our stock owing to the rush of orders.

But in order to meet your demand, we would recommend an excellent substitute. It is as good as the inquired good in quality, but the price is 25% lower. It has already found a market in Asia. We are deadly sure it will meet with warm reception in your area.

We look forward to hearing from you soon.

Yours sincerely,

Bert

尊敬的汤姆：

收到您于11月18号的来函，我们非常高兴。您询问是否还有宏基B-123型电脑，但是很遗憾地告诉贵公司，由于接到大批的订单，我方已无存货。

但为了满足您的需求，我方可推荐给您一款与B-123型电脑差不多的替代品。它的质量和原先的产品一样好，但是价格却便宜25%。它在亚洲有很大的市场，我们确信它在当地也会受到热捧的。

期待您的早日回复。

伯特 谨上

读书笔记

范例 6 | 询问交货日期

Dear Sir or Madam,

I'm writing to confirm the order of March 20th (Order No.123) we placed to you. Would you like to inform us how long it will take you to make the delivery.

These computers are planned to transport to Wuhan. Now, only 15 days are left. So we hope you could understand our situation.

Your company enjoys an excellent reputation, maybe something is wrong with the physical distribution. We really want a definite date of the delivery. Moreover, please mail us the invoice.

Yours sincerely,

Bruce

敬启者：

我方来信是确认在3月20号公司下的订单123。烦请告诉我方，这批货物要多久才能到货。

这批电脑是打算送去武汉的。现在离截止日只有15天了。我方希望贵公司能理解我们现在的情形。

获悉贵公司在业内享有盛誉，也许是物流上出了问题。但我们迫切需要一个确切的交货日期。同时，请将发票送到本公司。

布鲁斯 谨上

读书笔记

邮件回复 *Reply*

Dear Bruce,

We have received your letter of May 3rd and note that you have booked our products. Our confirmation of the order will be forwarded to you in few days.

I'm quite aware that it's of great importance to our buyers that the arrival date of this order should be arranged as early as possible. But recently, we have received a great amount of orders. We regret that we have to delay the schedule delivery date to June 5th.

On another hand, in order to keep the high quality of our products, I hope you could understand us.

Your understanding will be appreciated.

Yours truly,

Byrne

尊敬的布鲁斯：

我方已收到你方5月3日的来信，并获悉你已订购我们的产品。对订单的确认过些日子会发给你。

我方非常清楚交货日期对买方的重要性，交货越快越好。但最近，我们收到大批订单。我方不得不延长交货日期到6月5号。

另外，也为了保证产品质量。希望贵公司能理解我们。

如能得到体谅，我方将不胜感激。

伯恩 谨上

读书笔记

范例 7 | 询问价格及运费

Dear Sir or Madam,

We acknowledge receipt of both your offer of May 5th and the samples of women's shirts, for which we extend our sincere gratitude.

While appreciating the good quality and design of your shirts, we find your price is rather high for the market we wish to supply, because our market is mainly open to the middle-class.

We have also to point out that women's shirts are available in our market from several European manufacturers, all of which are at price from 15% to 20% below yours.

Such being the case, we have to ask you to consider if you can make reduction in your price, saying 10%. As our order would be around 50,000 yuan, you may think it worthwhile to make a concession.

In addition, we would like to enquire the freight and insurance to Wuhan.

Your immediate reply will be appreciated.

Yours faithfully,

John Smith

敬启者：

很高兴收到你方5月5号的报价和女式衬衫的样品，十分感谢。

虽然贵公司的产品质量和设计都是上层，但是您的报价对我们市场来说相对较高，因为我们的市场主要是面向中产阶级。

还有一点需指出的是，也有一些欧洲的制造商在我们市场上销售这样的女式衬衫，他们的价格比你的低10%~20%。

所以，我方请你方考虑一下能否在价格上做一些退让，给我们打9折。我们的订单也有5万元，你方做一点让步也是值得的。

此外，我们想知道到武汉的运费和保险费是多少。

期待您的及时回复。

约翰·斯密斯 谨上

邮件回复 *Reply*

Dear Smith,

We learn from your letter of March 3rd that our price for the subject article is found to be on the high side.

Much as we could like to cooperate with you in expanding sales, we must say frankly that we are unable to grant the reduction you asked for.

The quantity you require is only 500 pieces, if you can increase it to 1,000 pieces; we may consider allowing you a 10% reduction.

As for the freight, we enclose a detailed price list about different kinds of transportation.

Please be assured that we shall do our best to assist you in selling the products. We hope we can conclude the deal at an early date.

Yours sincerely,

Tom Hanson

尊敬的史密斯先生：

从您3月3号的来信获悉，您觉得我们的报价有点高。

虽然我们愿一起合作来扩大销售，但坦率说我们不能按你的要求降价。

贵公司只订购了500件，如果您能加大订购量至1000件，我们会考虑给你10%的折扣。

至于运费问题，我已经随函附上各种运输方式的报价表。

请放心我们会尽力协助你们推销该产品，希望我们早日达成生意。

汤姆·汉森 谨上

读书笔记

范例 8 | 询问未到货商品

Dear Mr. Liu,

I'm writing to inquire the information about the sports shoes we ordered on April 15th. Concerning our order No.32 for 1,000 pairs of sports shoes, you have delivered only 500 pairs on May 5th. Another 500 pairs are much overdue.

As a result, we can't keep our promise that we could supply by the end of May to the customers, thus causing us considerable difficulties. Please give us a reasonable explanation and do everything possible to ensure the shipment before May 15th. Please inform us by return when you can ship with certainty so that we can promise the responsible time of delivery to our customers who are proposing to cancel this order.

I hope you could deal with this problem seriously and give us an early reply.

We look forward to hearing from you in the near future.

Yours sincerely,

Mike

尊敬的刘先生：

我想询问我方于4月15号订购的运动鞋的信息。本公司第32号订单订购的1000双运动鞋，贵方至今只于5月5日交付了500双，尚有500双逾期甚久未交。

此事导致的结果就是我们不能兑现向顾客许下的关于保证在5月底交货的承诺，因此造成了我们极大的困扰。请贵方给我们一个合理的解释并尽一切可能在5月15日之前装货。请你方将可以交货的确切时间告知我方，以便向威胁我方取消订货的客户保证交货时间。

希望你方能严肃处理此事，快速给予答复。

期待您的早日回复。

迈克 谨上

邮件回复 *Reply*

Dear Mike,

We are sorry that the goods you ordered have not been delivered on time. Please accept our sincere apologies.

It's a result of a unavoidable difficulties with our own raw material suppliers, and with a defective machine, which has now been repaired but causes a disorder in production.

We have taken strenuous measures to assure that we could guarantee the punctual shipment.

We hope you could understand our situation. Since we value your business, we would like to offer you a 10% discount for your next orders with us.

We look forward to hearing from you.

Yours truly,

Liu Qin

尊敬的迈克：

没有按期交付您所订的货物，我们感到非常抱歉。请接受我们真诚的道歉。

导致这次事件的原因是我们遇到不可以避免的困难，因为我们的原材料供应商出了问题，而且出现了机器故障，虽然已修复却影响了生产的工序。

我们已经竭尽全力确保准时交货。

希望贵方能理解我方的处境。我方非常珍惜和贵方合作的机会，在下一次的合作中我们会给你方10%的折扣。

期待您的早日回复。

刘沁 谨上

读书笔记

范例 9 | 询问仓库租赁

Dear Sir or Madam,

We have been informed by Wuhan Food Company that you have many spare warehouses for renting. Our company is interested in leasing a huge warehouse to reserve our products shipped from South America.

Please inform us of the detailed information about the lease, including the total area of the warehouse and its payment requirements. In addition, please tell us its location, so that we can arrange the physical distribution.

It will be appreciated if you could send us the picture of the warehouse.

Your immediate reply will be appreciated.

Yours truly,

Jim

敬启者：

我方从武汉食品公司得知贵公司有许多正待出租的仓库。本公司希望租下一个大仓库来存放我们从南美运来的货物。

敬请告诉我们有关租赁的详细信息，包括仓库的总面积和付款的要求。此外，也请告知仓库的具体位置，方便我们安排运货。

如有条件，请您能附上一张仓库照片，我将不胜感激。

期待您的早日回复。

吉姆 谨上

读书笔记

邮件回复 *Reply*

Dear Jim,

Thanks for your letter of May 5th, inquiring the information about our warehouses. Actually, we are also looking for partner.

We are pleased to enclose the picture of our warehouses and the price list of warehouses of different areas. Besides, we have drawn map showing their location.

We look forward to cooperating with you.

Yours truly,

Sam

尊敬的吉姆：

感谢您于5月5号来函询问我们仓库租赁问题。实际上，我们也在找合作伙伴。

随函附上仓库的照片以及不同面积仓库的价目表。另外，我们也附上地图一张。

期待与贵公司的合作。

萨姆 谨上

读书笔记

范例 10 | 对产品价格的疑问（标价和实收价不符）

Dear Mr. Green,

We have received the contract you sent us. After reading through it, we find that the quotation marked on the contract is not in accordance with the pervious quotation you offered us.

You told us you would give us an allowance, which cutting the price by 2%. But the contract indicates you sell the goods to us at its original price, which makes us confused. We are informed that your company enjoys an excellent reputation in your area. Therefore, we believe that you won't play a joke with us, something must be wrong.

Besides, due to this problem we are unable to sign our name on it. You should confirm the contract again and then give us a definite reply.

Your immediate attention to this matter will be greatly appreciated.

Yours truly,

Peter

尊敬的格林先生：

本公司已收到贵方寄来的合同。但我方发现合同上的标价与您之前的报价不一致。

贵公司答应给我方低于价格的2%为优惠。但合同表明还是按原价售予本公司，这不得不让我们感到困惑。贵公司在业内享有盛誉，应该不会跟我方开这样的玩笑，一定有什么误会。

而且，由于这个原因，我方不能在合同上签字。请贵方再核对一下合同以便给我们一个确切的答复。

盼速回。

彼得 谨上

邮件回复 *Reply*

Dear Peter,

Thank you for your inquiry of 25 May, 2010. We regret to tell you that we have increased our prices at present.

Because we are paying 10% more for our raw material than that we were paying last year. Some of our subcontractors have raised their prices by as much as 15%.

As you know, we take great pride in our machines and are jealous of the reputation for quality and dependability which we have achieved over the last 40 years. We will not compromise that reputation because of rising costs; we have therefore decided to raise the price of some of our machines.

We hope you will understand our position and look forward to your orders.

Yours truly,

Green

尊敬的彼得：

感谢您于2010年5月25日的来函，抱歉的是，目前我们已调高了产品价格。

这次调整原因是原材料价格上涨10%，一些承包商的价格调升15%。

过去40年，本公司生产的机器质量优良，性能可靠。现在由于成本上升，为确保产品质量，我们决定上调价格。

上述情况，还望理解。愿能与贵公司保持合作。

格林 谨上

读书笔记

范例 11 | 对商品送达日期的疑问

Dear Sir or Madam:

With reference to our order No.123 of May 5th.We shall be glad to know when we may expect delivery, as they are urgently required.

When we made the initial inquiry, your department assured us that delivery would only take a month, and we placed the order on that understanding as we wished to have the shoes before the end of November. Your delay in delivery has caused us great inconvenience.

Will you please inform us by fax or e-mail of the earliest possible date when you can deliver these goods? Should the delay be longer than two or three weeks, we shall regretfully have to cancel the order.

We are looking forward to your early reply.

Yours truly,

Jack

尊敬的先生/女士：

请贵公司告知我方的订货（单号123）什么时候才能到货，因为我方急需这批货物。

我方第一次询问时，贵方向本公司保证在一个月内到货。我方也是以为在11月就可拿到货才向贵公司下订单的。而现在的延迟交货给我们带来了很大的不便。

请告知我方贵公司最快的送货日期。如果两三个星期内还不交货，我方就考虑撤销订单了。

盼早日回复。

杰克 谨上

读书笔记

邮件回复 Reply

Dear Jack,

We are in receipt of your letter of 1st June and very much regret the delay in delivering the above. We are now making the arrangement for immediate delivery, which means you will have your goods before the end of June.

The main factor contributing to the delay is that we haven't found an appropriate shipper until last week. At any rate, your goods have been shipped safely. They are supposed to arrive on June 3rd.

We apologize for any inconvenience.

Yours truly,

Smith

尊敬的杰克：

已收到您于6月1号的来函。我方对未能及时交货表示抱歉。我方现在已为及时交货做好准备。您在月底前就可以收到货。

导致这次延误的主要原因是，上个星期我们才找到合适的船舶公司。无论如何，您的货物已安全装运，6月3号就可到达。

我们为给贵公司带来的不便表示歉意。

史密斯 谨上

读书笔记

范例 12 | 对合约内容的疑问

Dear Sir or Madam,

We are writing to inquire information about the contract we signed last month. Here are some items of the contract,

Commodity: Men's T-shirts.

Specification: S/3, M/6, L/3

Colors: white, blue, green and yellow

Quantity: 6,000 dozen

Packing: 10 dozen in a box

Shipment: May

Terms of payment: irrevocable letter of credit by draft at sight

We found that shipment is unclear. Would you please tell us the definite date of shipment?

Your prompt reply is welcome.

Yours faithfully,

Jake

敬启者:

就上月与贵公司签订的合同，我方想再咨询一下相关事宜。以下是合同部分条款:

商品：男式T恤

规格：S/3, M/6, L/3

颜色：白、蓝、绿、黄

数量：72000件

包装；一盒120件

装运期：5月

付款方式：不可撤销即期信用证

我方发现装运期限不明确。请贵公司给我方一个确切的日期。

望速回。

杰克 谨上

读书笔记

邮件回复 *Reply*

Dear Jake,

We acknowledge your letter dated 3rd May, inquiring about shipment.

When we offered the consignment, it was clearly stated that we would make delivery of the goods on May 20th. If you request to advance the shipment, what we can do at best is to ship them in part on May 15th and the remaining 3,000 dozen on June 1st. We hope the proposal will satisfy you. Should the arrangement be accepted, you are under the necessity of amendment of the covering credit to allow partial shipments and meanwhile informing us.

The earlier confirmation from you is appreciated.

Yours truly,

Mike

尊敬的杰克：

已收到您于5月3号关于装运期的询函。

在我们委任托运时就告知贵方装运期为5月20号。如果贵公司想提前的话，我方只能分期转运，第一批于5月15号装货，剩余的36000件将于6月1号装货。如果接受转运，请提供相关信誉担保并通知我们。

盼尽早回复。

迈克 谨上

读书笔记

范例 13 | 对商品退换时间的疑问

Dear Mr. David,

We have received the skirts we ordered last month. However, the color of the skirts is a bit lighter than the samples you sent us and they are not what we expected, which make us disappointed. Therefore, we would like to return these goods. Would you please tell us when we shall send them back?

Meanwhile, would you mind us exchanging them for darker ones, which are the same with the samples? We learn from our last negotiation that you only take the responsibility of returning in 7 days since the goods have been sent. I wonder if you have sufficient goods for exchanging at present. We would like to send the goods back at your convenience.

Your immediate attention to this problem will be appreciated.

Yours sincerely,

Frank

尊敬的戴维：

我方已收到订购的裙子。但是，裙子的颜色比贵方之前寄送的样品颜色浅，也不是我们所期待的那样。这令我方非常失望。因此我们希望退还这批物品。可以告诉我们具体的退换时间吗？

同时，我方想换一批颜色深一点、和样品颜色一样的货可以吗。从上次谈判得知，贵公司只在发送货物后的7天内负责退换。我方想了解贵方是否有足够的存货来交换。我方愿在贵方方便的时候进行退换。

对于您的及时回复，我方将不胜感激。

弗兰克 谨上

读书笔记

邮件回复 Reply

Dear Mr. Frank,

We are very sorry to learn from your letter of May 4th that you are dissatisfied about the skirts we sent. To begin with, we apologize for our mistakes. In response to your enquiry, we regret to tell you that the skirts you expect have been sold out. We have no stock of skirts at present.

However, we are making effort to increase the daily output to meet your demand. We believe that we can entertain your enquiry by the end of the month.

We would like to take the losses. If you have any questions, please let us know.

Yours truly,

David

尊敬的弗兰克先生：

从您5月4号的来函获悉，贵公司不太满意我方的寄来的货物。我们对此表示歉意。至于您所提出的退换条件，很遗憾地告诉贵公司，你方所期望的那款裙子已经售完。目前，我方已无库存所剩。

但是，我们正努力增加日产量来满足您的需求。我方确信在这个月底就能给您换货。

我方愿承担所有损失。如还有问题，请联系我们。

戴维 谨上

读书笔记

范例 14 | 对商品配送标准的疑问

Dear Sir or Madam,

We are in receipt of your letter of April 6th informing us that the goods have been prepared.

With regard to the packing of knives, you may say that you have taken up the matter with the competent departments and are of the opinion that packing in cartons will well protect against moisture. They are light and convenient to handle. However, we are of the opinion that if the result of packing in cartons turned out to the satisfaction of our clients, you may continue using this packing in the future.

Meanwhile, we wonder if they exceed an overall length of 1 meter. All cartons should be marked as usual, but please number them consecutively from No.1 to No.5. It will be appreciated if you could tell us the detailed information about the packing.

Yours,

James

尊敬的先生/女士：

4月6号，贵公司来函告知货物已准备装运。

对于刀的包装，贵方建议用盒装可以预防潮湿。这样也方便操作。如果客户对此包装表示满意的话，您可以继续使用该包装。

此外，请告知我们包装盒的长度是否超过一米。所有包装箱必须照常加以标志，将号码从1到5连续编号。若能告诉我们关于包装的详细信息将不胜感激。

詹姆斯 谨上

读书笔记

邮件回复 *Reply*

Dear James,

In reply to your letter of 16th April inquiring about packing of our knives. We desire to state as bellow:

Our exported knives are packed in boxes of one dozen each, 100 boxes to carton. The dimensions are 17cm high, 30cm wide and 50cm long with a volume of about 0.026 cubic-meter. The gross weight is 23.5kg while the net weight is 22.5kg.

And the wording "Made in China" is also stenciled on the package. Should you have any special preference in this respect, please let us know and we will meet you to the best of our ability.

We thank you in advance for your early reply.

Yours truly,

Wang Lin

尊敬的詹姆斯：

回复您于4月16号的关于刀的包装的询函，我们的描述如下：

每盒12把，100盒一个包装箱；尺寸是17厘米高，30厘米宽，50厘米长；容积为0.026立方米，毛重23.5千克，净重22.5千克。

"中国制造"的字样也印在包装箱上面。如果贵方在这方面还有什么建议，我们愿尽一切协助你们。

提前对您的回复表示感谢。

王林 谨上

读书笔记

范例 15 | 对商品折扣的疑问

Dear Sir or Madam,

Thank you for your brochure for electronic calculator and the photo booklet enclosed.

We have approached a number of our customers in this area and many of them take an interest in these types of calculator. We therefore ask you to give us your best offer.

We learn that your product retails for $30.00. Is there a trade discount for about 80 units and reorders in perhaps lots of 20?

We look forward to your early reply.

Yours sincerely,

Tom

尊敬的先生/女士：

感谢贵公司给我们寄来的电子计算器的小册子以及相册。

我找过很多当地的消费者他们中很多人对这款计算器很感兴趣。因此请给我方您最合理的报价。

贵公司的该类产品零售价是30美元.如果我们订购 80台有优惠的吗，再订购20台呢?

盼早日回复。

汤姆 谨上

邮件回复 *Reply*

Dear Mr. Tom,

We are in receipt of your letter of May 5th. After careful consideration, we offer a discount of 10 percent on orders of 40 or more calculators. I have enclosed an order bank for your convenience.

The enclosed catalogue gives complete details about service, warranties. Actually, a carrying case is not necessary because its exterior leather can protect it and make it convenient to take.

Thank you for inquiring about the discount.

Yours truly,

Rose

尊敬的 汤姆先生:

我方已收到您5月5号的来信，仔细考虑后，如果您的订购量达40台以上，我们给打9折。为了您的方便，我方提供支付行。

附件目录详细的描述了服务保修的细节。事实上，计算机并不需要包装箱，它外面的皮革即能保护它也使它拿起来更加轻便。

感谢您的来函询问。

罗斯 谨上

范例 16 | 对工作职责的疑问

Dear Sir or Madam,

In response to your advertisement in the newspaper of Jan.15th, I wish to apply for the position of manager assistant. Would you please send me more detailed information about this post?

As I have heard about your company for a long time, you are the leading exporter company in our area. Now, it's a good chance for me to realize my dream.

I enclose a copy of my resume and three copies of my certifications.

Yours sincerely,

Tom

尊敬的先生/女士：

贵公司在1月15号，在报纸上刊登招聘经理助理。现拟应征。但是，对于助理的职责问题，我不太清楚。烦请您告知我该职位的详细信息。

很久前就听说贵公司是我地的出口商的领头羊。现在正是一个好的机会。

随函附上我的简历和相关的证书。

汤姆 谨上

邮件回复 Reply

Dear Tom,

With reference to your letter of Monday 12 April, I'm pleased to tell you that we are satisfied with your qualifications. We have enclosed detailed information about the responsibility of the assistant. Meanwhile, an interview has been scheduled for you on Monday, May 5th, 2020 at 10 clock with Mr. Peter, head of personnel; his office is located on the 10th floor.

If you are unable to keep this appointment or if you have any questions, please call me at 123456.

Yours,

Mary

尊敬的汤姆：

就你4月12号（星期一）的来信，我们对你的个人简历非常满意。我已附上关于助理一职的详细信息。同时，我们为你准备了一次面试，时间为2020年5月5号星期一上午10点，面试官是负责人事的皮特，他的办公室在10层。

如果不能赴约或还有其他问题，请拨123456与我联系。

玛丽 谨上

Unit 11 请求篇

（1）如何写

a）写信包括提出请求并说明原因；建议的时间和地点等；请对方回复。

b）回信分为接受和拒绝两种。接受一般包括：表明来信收悉并接受；重述具体时间、地点等；表示希望或感谢。拒绝一般包括：表明来信收悉；说明拒绝的原因；致歉。

（2）实用例句

a）Thank you for your letter of 7th May regarding your new product.

5月7日有关新产品的函收悉。

b）I leave it to you to choose.

听你的选择。

c）I look forward to seeing you again.

期待与您再见面。

d）I am planning a trip to France next month, and I am looking forward to meeting you.

下月我将赴法国一游，期望能与您会面。

e）Please let me know when you would like to call on us.

望告知您方何时将要造访我司。

f）Could you choose a place for the meeting?

能否选定会面地点？

g）We will keep you informed on our progress and look forward to hearing from you.

愿进一步加强联系，并候复音。

h）If for any reason you are unable to attend, please call me so that we can make other arrangements.

若因故不能出席，烦请致电告知，以便另行安排。

范例 1 | 请求提供公司资料

Dear Mrs. Liu,

I've been trying to get information on a company in Wuhan called ABC Corporation. I watched their products in the Guangzhou Fair but I've had difficulty finding much information on the company. I've tried several standard sources on the Internet but with little luck.

Would you have access to an annual report or any other type of information that would help me better understand the company and its operation? I'm especially interested in their overall financial health and future performance. I'm assuming you have access to information sources that are beyond my reach.

I appreciate your assistance.

Yours sincerely,

Zhou Feng

尊敬的刘先生：

我一直试图了解武汉一家名为ABC公司的信息。我在广交会上看到过他们的展品，但是很难收集到有关他们公司的信息。我试过利用网络上常见的信息渠道来了解，但是效果不佳。

您有办法得到他们的年度报告或是其他有助于我了解该公司及其运作的信息吗？我对他们的整体财务状况及未来发展前景非常感兴趣。我相信您一定有我所没有的信息渠道。

期待您的帮助。

周峰 敬上

邮件回复 *Reply*

Dear Mr. Zhou,

I have received your letter, asking for the information on ABC Corporation.

I should have helped you, but I regret that I will be unable, because I recently retired from my post. But I suggest you contact my former colleague, Mr. Gong, who is also an expert in investigating companies' financial status. You can get him at 18976326544.

Yours sincerely,

Liu Ming

亲爱的周先生：

我收到了您要求了解ABC公司信息的来信。

我本来应该帮助你，但是最近我从岗位上退了下来，所以爱莫能助。但是我向你推荐我以前的同事龚先生，他也是调查公司财务状况的专家。他的电话是18976326544。

刘明 敬上

范例 2 | 请求订购办公用品

Dear Mr. Li,

Our department has recently recruited two new staff members, and we need to provide them with the necessary office supplies. We, on behalf of them, hereby apply for two Lenovo desktop computers with an amount of ￥7,000.

We are looking forward to your approval.

Research and Development Section

尊敬的李先生：

我部最近来了两名新同事，需为他们提供必要的办公用品。特此申请购置联想台式电脑两台，金额7000元整。

期待获得您的批准。

研发部

邮件回复 *Reply*

Research and Development Section,

Your application for two Lenovo desktop computers for new staff members has been approved. You need to come to the Property Center to fill in a form.

Li Zhong

研发部：

你部关于为新进员工购置两台联想台式电脑的申请已经批复同意。请于资产管理处填写表格一份。

李忠

读书笔记

范例 3 | 请求付款

Dear Mr. Davis,

Our records show that you have an outstanding balance dating back to March, 2019. Your March invoice was for ￥5,000 and we have not received this payment. Please find a copy of the invoice enclosed.

If this amount has already been paid, please disregard this notice. Otherwise, please forward us the amount owed in full by May 1st, 2019. As our contract indicates, we begin charging 5% interest for any outstanding balances after 30 days.

Thank you in advance for your cooperation. We hope to continue doing business with you in the future.

Yours sincerely,

John Anderson

亲爱的戴维斯先生：

我们的记录表明您2019年3月的账务。您3月的发货单金额为5000元，我们目前还没有收到这笔账目。附件请查收发货单附件一份。

如果这笔账目已经支付，那么请忽视本次提醒。否则，请您在2019年5月1日前将所付款项全额支付给我们。按照我们的合同规定，我们将对超过30天未清的账目收取5%的利息。

我们预先对您的合作表示感谢。我们希望今后继续和您合作做生意。

约翰·安德森 敬上

读书笔记

邮件回复 *Reply*

Dear Mr. Anderson,

We acknowledge with apology receipt of your letter April 15, 2019, requesting payment of our March invoice. We have to admit that this delay was due to our oversight, as we have been working to meet a deadline.

We are now arranging for the amount to be transferred to your account and you can expect to receive it in 24 hours.

We, again, extend our sincerest apology for the delay and the inconvenience it has caused to you.

Yours sincerely,

Thomas Davis

亲爱的安德森先生：

我们收到了你们2019年4月5日的来信，要求我们偿付3月份的发货账目，我们感到非常抱歉。我们必须承认，由于我们一直在赶着完成一个即将到期的任务，以致疏忽了这一点。

我们正在安排将款项划入你方账户，你们应该可在24小时内收到。

我们再次对付款延迟及其给你们带来的麻烦表示道歉。

汤姆 · 戴维斯 敬上

读书笔记

范例 4 | 请求购买回应

Dear Sir,

We wish to refer to our letter dated March 15, 2019.

Complying with your request, we have sent you our offer for those items quoted.

Since component parts and labor costs are increased, it is quite certain that other manufacturers will raise their price pretty soon.

In order to avoid the effect by the change of price, we shall be most appreciated if you could send us your purchasing order before the end of this month, so that we may stick on the previous price which we offered to you before.

Your prompt reply will be highly appreciated.

Yours sincerely,

ABC Company

尊敬的先生：

本公司曾于2019年3月15日奉上一函。

依照贵方指示，本公司已将有关款式价格报出。

由于配件与工资已经上涨，似乎可以断定其他厂商将于最近提高售价。

为了避免任何价格变更的影响，请于本月底前将贵公司的订单惠寄，我方当不胜感激。本公司仍可依照前次报出的同样价格售予贵公司。

期待贵方能早日恢复，不胜感激。

ABC公司 敬上

邮件回复 *Reply*

Dear Sir,

We acknowledge with thanks your letter of March 30.

We are pleased to place an order with you. Please send us a CIF proforma invoice for 50 sets of Model 7869 the soonest possible so that we will be able to open the L/C for the order.

Enclosed please find an order confirmation.

Yours sincerely,

BBC Company

尊敬的先生：

我们很感谢你方3月30日的来函。

我们很高兴向你方下订单。请尽快寄送50台7869型产品到岸价形式发票一份，以便我们开具信用证。

附件请查收订单确认书。

BBC公司 敬上

范例 5 | 请求配送到家

Dear Sir,

I watched your commercial about the wheelchair on the Internet and I am badly in need of one, because I recently broke my left leg. I am quite interested in Model 3456, as it looks comfortable and lightweight. Since I live alone, I want to know whether you provide home delivery service or not. My address is as follows:

12 Lianhu Road, Hanyang District, Wuhan

I will appreciate your early reply.

Yours sincerely,

Tom Smith

尊敬的先生：

我在网上看到了你们的轮椅广告。我最近摔断了左腿，非常需要一辆。我对3456型号非常感兴趣，它看起来舒适而轻便。由于我是一个人居住，我想问一下你们是否能够提供送货上门的服务。我的地址是：

武汉市汉阳区莲湖路12号

期待你们早日回复。

汤姆·史密斯 敬上

邮件回复 *Reply*

Dear Mr. Smith,

We are sorry for the accident, and we hope you didn't hurt seriously.

Generally speaking, we do not provide home delivery for our customers. However, we will be delighted to make an exception this time in view of your situation.

You can place an order on the Internet, and we will arrange the delivery in two days.

Yours sincerely,

BBC Company

亲爱的史密斯先生：

我们对于您的意外受伤感到难过，希望您没有伤得很严重。

一般来说，我们是不提供送货上门服务的。但是，鉴于您的特殊情况，我们很乐意破一次例。

您可以在网上下一个订单，我们将在两天内安排送货。

BBC公司 敬上

范例 6 | 请求开具发票

Dear Sirs,

We have a client who requests us to obtain from you a proforma invoice for the following:

"SEAGULL" Brand Household Electric Heater Model 220

Please send us your CIF proforma invoice by fax and hard copy in quadruplicate by airmail for 500 sets of the above article the soonest possible so as to enable us to get our client's confirmation.

There is no question of our obtaining the import license. As soon as the license is approved, an L/C will be opened in your favor.

Your prompt attention to this matter will be highly appreciated.

Yours faithfully,

ETT Company

尊敬的先生们：

我们有一位客户要求我们向你方索要以下商品的形式发票：

"海鸥"牌220型号家用电热器。

请尽快以传真形式发送500台以上商品的到岸价形式发票，并以航邮形式发送一式四份复印件，以便我们的客户确认。

我们能够保证申请到进口许可证。一旦许可证获批，我们会开具以你方为受益人的信用证。

如蒙你方及时关照，我方将不胜感激。

ETT 公司 敬上

读书笔记

邮件回复 *Reply*

Dear Sirs,

We thank you for your letter of April 15, asking for a proforma invoice for 500 sets of "SEAGULL" Brand Household Electric Heater Model 220.

Complying with your request, we sent you the CIF proforma invoice by fax and will soon airmail the hard copy in quadruplicate, which you can expect to receive in one week.

Since you will have to apply for an import license for your order, we have made up the invoice to expire on June 20.

Yours sincerely,

BBC Company

尊敬的先生们：

感谢你方4月15日的来函，要求开具500台“海鸥”牌220型号家用电热器的形式发票。

应你方的要求，我们已经将到岸价形式发票通过传真形式发送你方，并且立刻就会将一式四份复印件航邮给你方，你方应该能够在一周内收到。

考虑到你方需要申请进口许可证，我们将发票的作废日期设在6月20日。

BBC公司 敬上

读书笔记

范例 7 | 请求变更日期

Dear Sir,

As stipulated in our contract No. 34567, shipment could be made in May provided your L/C reached us not later than April 15. However, we received your L/C only yesterday and it is absolutely impossible for us to ship the goods in May.

Under the circumstances, we regret to have to ask you to extend the above L/C to June 15, and accordingly, the date of shipment to June 30.

We will appreciate it if you can send us the amendment before May 15; otherwise shipment will be further postponed.

Yours faithfully,

GTT Company

尊敬的先生：

我们之间编号为34567的合同规定，如果你方能够在4月15日前提供信用证，我们就能保证5月份装船。但是，我们昨天才收到你们的信用证，所以5月份装船是绝不可能的。

在这种情况下，我们很抱歉不得不要求将上述信用证展期至6月15日，装船日期相应延期至6月30日。

如果你们能够在5月15日之前将修改后的信用证寄送给我们，我们当不胜感激；否则装船日期将再次延后。

GGT公司 敬上

邮件回复 *Reply*

Dear Sir,

We acknowledge receipt of your letter dated May 10th, asking for an extension of our L/C.

Complying with your request, we have made an application with our bank for the amendment, which you can expect to obtain in a week.

We look forward to your notice of shipment the soonest possible.

Yours sincerely,

FFT Company

尊敬的先生：

我们收到你方5月10日要求信用证展期的信件。

应你方的要求，我们已经向银行递交申请要求修改信用证，你们可以在一周之内收到上述信用证。

我们希望尽快收到你方的装运通知单。

FFT公司 敬上

范例 8 | 请求更换货品

Dear Sir,

Six cartons of the vases that we received from you on March 12, 2020 pursuant to our purchase order No.1234, were either broken or chipped upon delivery.

We would appreciate it if you would arrange for the replacement of the damaged items and advise us how you wish to handle the return of the broken merchandise.

Yours faithfully,

Tom Smith

尊敬的先生:

我方于2020年3月12日收到的编号为1234的订单货物中有六箱花瓶有破损。

请你方安排更换破损货品，并告知我方以何种方式退回损坏的货物，我方当不胜感激。

汤姆 · 史密斯 敬上

邮件回复 *Reply*

Dear Mr. Smith,

We acknowledge your letter dated Match 15, requesting the replacement of the broken and chipped vases. We are sorry for the damage. However, we can assure you, that all the goods were in perfect condition when they left here; hence, we are apparently not liable for the damage and would advise you to claim on the shipping company who should be responsible.

At any rate, we deeply regret to learn from you about this unfortunate incident and should it be necessary we shall be pleased to take the matter up on your behalf with the shipping company concerned.

Yours faithfully,

John Smith

亲爱的史密斯先生:

你方3月15日要求更换破损花瓶的来函收悉。我方对此表示遗憾。但是我方可以保证，所有货物离开此地时状况完好。因此，我方不能对货物损坏负责，我们建议你方向装运公司提出索赔，因为他们应对此事负责。

无论如何，发生这种不幸之事确实令人感到遗憾。如有必要，我们愿代你方与装运公司洽谈此事。

约翰 · 史密斯 敬上

范例 9 | 请求退货

Dear Sir,

I placed an online order with you last Friday evening, and the coat arrived today. When I opened the parcel, I was disappointed to discover that the color was totally different from what you displayed on the webpage. I am rejecting the coat and requesting that you refund the sum paid to you of ¥150.

I am looking forward to your early reply.

Yours faithfully,

Lu Ming

尊敬的先生：

我于上周五晚上在线下单订购了一件外套，今天收到了。打开包裹之后，我很遗憾地发现衣服的颜色和网页上呈现的完全不同。我要求退货并全额返还我支付的150元货款。

期待您的回复。

陆明 敬上

邮件回复 *Reply*

Dear Mr. Lu,

We regret our inability to grant your request to return the coat. As we have stated on our web, the color of the coat may seem slightly different from what is shown on the webpage. Hence, we are not responsible for returning goods for that reason.

Yours sincerely,

Zhang Yi

亲爱的陆先生：

我们很抱歉不能答应您退还外套的请求。正如我们网上声明中提到的那样，外套的颜色与网页上显示的有些许差异。因此，我们不支持此种理由退货。

张一 敬上

范例 10 | 请求退款

Dear Sir or Madam,

The Super Mincer FD3001 I purchased from you on May 15, 2020 turned out to be quite a disappointment. While it looked the same as the one I saw in your commercial, it did not perform in the same way.

Following the instructions, I placed an onion in its proper position and pushed down on the mincer, which immediately bent out of shape. I experienced the same problem when I attempted to dice a carrot.

Therefore, I am returning the Super Mincer FD3001 to you and asking that you issue me a full refund. I am not interested in receiving a replacement.

Yours sincerely,

Linda Smith

尊敬的先生/女士：

我于2020年5月15日从你处购买了一台型号为FD3001的超级料理机，结果令人非常沮丧。其外观和广告上一样，但是功能却大相径庭。

按照说明书上的指示，我将一个洋葱放在正确的位置，按下搅拌键后，机器立刻变形了。当我尝试着搅碎胡萝卜时，发生了同样的故障。

因此，我将这台型号为FD3001的超级料理机退还给你们，并且要求你们全额退款。我对更换货品不感兴趣。

琳达·史密斯 敬上

邮件回复 *Reply*

Dear Ms. Smith,

We acknowledge your letter of March 30, 2020, and feel sorry for the inconvenience you experienced. When we receive the mincer you returned, we will refund you the sum you paid for it.

We express our sincere apology again.

Yours sincerely,

BBC Company

尊敬的史密斯女士：

您2020年3月30日的来函我们收悉，我们为给您带来的不便表示抱歉。我们收到退回的料理机后就会给您办理全额退款。

再次向您表达我们最诚挚的歉意。

BBC公司 敬上

范例 11 | 请求推荐客户

Dear Mr. Chen,

As far as you know, ABC Company is gaining ground.

Since you have expressed that you are very satisfied with our service, I wonder if you could strongly recommend some potential clients to us for activating our business.

We deeply appreciate any suggestions you would offer.

Yours sincerely,

Tom Smith

亲爱的陈先生：

正如您所知，ABC公司正在发展壮大。

既然您曾经表示，对我公司提供的服务非常满意，那么我想知道您是否能推荐一些潜在的客户来帮助我们扩展业务呢？

如果您能提供任何建议，我们将非常感谢。

汤姆·史密斯 敬上

邮件回复 *Reply*

Dear Mr. Smith,

I have received your letter of March 30, 2020. I am very delighted to recommend our business partner BBC Company, who is a major importer of garments in Europe. You can contact them at 0044-28-56781234.

Yours sincerely,

Chen Lei

尊敬的史密斯先生：

我收到了您2020年3月30日的来信。我很乐意向您推荐我们的合作伙伴BBC公司，他们是欧洲地区的主要成衣进口商。您可以通过电话0044—28—56781234与他们取得联系。

陈雷 敬上

范例 12 | 请求追加投资

Dear Mr. Zhou,

I am very glad to inform you that ABC Company runs quite well since its establishment. However, we are now meeting a big fiscal challenge because of the fiercely global financial crisis. So I would like to know if it is possible for you to make additional investment to help us pull through the current difficulty.

Thank you so much for your careful consideration and we expect your support!

Yours faithfully,

Huang Gang

ABC Corporation

亲爱的周先生：

我很高兴地告知您，ABC公司自开业以来运营状况良好。但是，由于最近全球金融危机的恶劣影响，我们现在面临着巨大的财政困难。因此，我想知道你们能否追加投资帮助我们渡过目前的难关。

非常感谢您的考虑，我们期待您的支持。

ABC公司

黄刚 敬上

邮件回复 *Reply*

Dear Mr. Huang,

Complying with your request of March 28, 2020, we hereby invest an additional ￥5,000,000 in the Mutual Term Deposits Fund.

Our cheque for the above amount is attached.

Yours sincerely,

Zhou Feng

尊敬的黄先生：

应你方2020年3月28日的请求，我方特追加500万人民币，存入共同的定期存款基金。

附件请查收上述金额支票。

周峰 敬上

范例 13 | 请求制定协议书

Dear Sir,

Thank you for your letter dated March 15, 2020 and the enclosed catalogue and price list. After careful study, we decide to order from you the items in it.

To avoid any possible disputes in the future, we request that you create an agreement, stipulating the specifications. If it is ready, please send us a copy. We will sign it and send it back to you so that you can execute our order as soon as possible.

Yours sincerely,

BBC Company

尊敬的先生：

感谢你方2020年3月15日的来信及所付产品目录及价格目录。经我方仔细研究，我们决定从你方订购目录上的货品。

为了避免将来产生纠纷，我方要求你方制定协议书，列出详细的条款。协议书制定好之后，请给我方寄送一份。我方签署之后寄还你方，以便你方能够尽早执行我方订单。

BBC公司 敬上

邮件回复 *Reply*

Dear Sirs,

We acknowledge with thanks your letter dated March 30, 2020.

Complying with your request, we have created an agreement regarding the transaction. Enclosed please find a copy of the agreement. Please put your signature on it and send it back to us the soonest possible.

Yours faithfully,

BTT Company

尊敬的先生：

我们非常感谢你方2020年3月30日的来信。

应你方要求，我们已经就此次交易制定了协议书。附件中请查收协议书一份。请你方尽快签署并寄还我方。

BTT公司 敬上

范例 14 | 请求返还协议书

Dear Mr. White,

Have you skimmed over the agreement and found everything in order? We didn't contact you until now, as you instructed us to wait for your response.

Could you send us a copy of the signed agreement as soon as possible? We are eager to open our business soon.

Looking forward to hearing from you soon.

Yours sincerely,

Tom Smith

尊敬的怀特先生：

你们是否已经过目协议并确认一切准备就绪呢？您告知我们等您的回复，所以我们一直没有和你联系。

您能否以最快速度把已经签署好的协议寄给我们？我们很希望能尽早开展业务。

期待您的回复！

汤姆·史密斯 敬上

邮件回复 *Reply*

Dear Mr. Smith,

We have received your letter dated on March 30, 2020. We apologize for our negligence for not being able to send you back the signed agreement in time. We have been busy in meeting a deadline.

We apologize again for the inconvenience this incident has caused you.

Enclosed please find the signed agreement.

Yours sincerely,

Brown White

亲爱的史密斯先生：

我们收到了您2020年3月30日的来信。我们很抱歉由于我们的疏忽没能及时寄还签署好的协议。我们一直在赶着一个即将到期的工程。

再次为此次事故为您造成的不便表示歉意。

附件请查收签好的协议。

布朗·怀特 敬上

范例 15 | 请求会面

Dear Mr. Atkinson,

It was a pleasure to speak with you the other day regarding how our *Magic lathe* can reduce your manufacturing costs by up to 30%. I believe that we can accomplish much if you, Mr. Huang and Professor Li meet for approximately one hour sometime this week. Our goal will be to determine whether the *Magic lathe* can interface with your existing manufacturing equipment.

I am available on April 11 to 15, any time before 4:30 p.m. When is most convenient for you and the others? Please contact me sometime tomorrow to confirm the date and time of our meeting.

I am looking forward to meeting with you soon.

Yours truly,

Tom Smith

尊敬的阿特金森先生：

我们很高兴改天能与您共同探讨如何利用我们的神奇牌车床将你们的生产成本降低30%以上的问题。如果本周您能抽出时间与黄先生和李教授进行约一个小时的面谈，我相信我们一定会收获颇丰的。我们的目标是要证明神奇牌车床是否能够与你们目前的生产设备对接。

4月11日至15日下午4:30前的任何时间我都可以会面。对于您和其他诸位什么时间比较方便呢？请于明天某一时间与我取得联系，确定具体会面的时间。

我期待与您尽早会面。

汤姆 · 史密斯 敬上

邮件回复 *Reply*

Dear Mr. Smith,

I have received your mail on April 8, suggesting a meeting to speak with some experts regarding your lathe, which I believe will benefit both parties. May I suggest April 13 at 3:00 p.m.?

Yours sincerely,

Adam Atkinson

尊敬的史密斯先生：

我收到了您4月8日的来信，建议就你们的车床与几个专家面谈。我觉得这是一个对双方都有利的事情。我建议4月13日下午3点，可以吗？

亚当 · 阿特金森 敬上

范例 16 | 请求协助

Dear Consumer Action Colum,

Three weeks ago I ordered a coat through the Internet, but it turned out to be a disappointment with a big hole in the pocket. I contacted with the seller, who refused to replace it or refund me for the reason that the defectiveness is invisible. I felt it hard to accept their way of disposing the matter.

I would appreciate your intervention and advice as to what I should do next.

Zhang Dan

尊敬的消费者行动栏目：

三个星期前我在网上订了一件外套，但结果发现外套口袋内有一个大洞。我联系了卖家，他们拒绝换货或是退款，理由是这种瑕疵从外面看不出来。我很难接受他们的处理方式。

我请求你们的干预，如能建议我下一步该怎么做，不胜感激。

张丹 敬上

邮件回复 *Reply*

Dear Ms. Zhang,

We received your mail of March 24, 2020. We suggest you call 315 to make a complaint and believe they will deal with the matter in a more satisfactory way.

Consumer Action Colum

亲爱的张女士：

我们收到了您2020年3月24日的邮件。我们建议您拨打315进行投诉，相信他们的处理方式会令您满意。

消费者行动栏目

范例 17 | 请求澄清事实

Dear Sir or Madam,

We are now seeking for a competent sales representative and one of the candidates is a man named Sandy Clark who claimed four months' internship as a sales person in your company. We hereby request your clarification of Mr. Clark's work experience in your company.

We will appreciate it if you can send us an early reply.

Yours sincerely,

BBC Company

尊敬的先生/女士：

我们正在招聘一名称职的销售代表，其中的一位应征者是一位名为桑迪·克拉克的男士，他自称曾在贵公司实习四个月。我们特此请求您为克拉克先生的工作经历澄清一下。

若您能尽早回复，将不胜感激。

BBC公司 敬上

邮件回复 *Reply*

Dear Sir or Madam,

This letter is in response to your request for clarification of Mr. Sandy Clark's internship in our company.

Mr. Sandy worked in our company as an intern sales person from June to October in 2010. He worked very hard, showing his potential talents to be a good salesman.

Yours sincerely,

ATT Company

尊敬的先生/女士：

这封信是用来回复您要求澄清桑迪·克拉克在我公司的实习情况的请求。

桑迪先生于2010年6月至10月在我公司做实习销售员。他工作十分努力，展示了自己成为一名成功销售员的潜在才能。

ATT公司 敬上

Unit 12 投诉篇

（1）如何写

投诉信是客户对所提供的服务或所购买的商品不满意时，向商家、机构提出相关的问题，并希望问题得到解决和处理所写的信件。这类信件的写作要点通常包括以下几方面：

a）对方的正式称谓，如某机构、某先生；

b）提出写信的目的是为了抱怨或投诉；

c）表明投诉的原因；

d）向对方表示希望问题能够得到解决的意愿；

e）留下自己的联系方式，以便能够得到回复。

（2）实用例句

a）I am writing to tell you I'm not satisfied with your service.

我写信是为了告诉你我不满意你的服务。

b）On inspection, we found that the quality of the goods did not meet the contract standard.

通过检验，我们发现货物的质量不符合合同规定标准。

c）A portion of the goods arrived damaged. We have to put in a claim for the damage.

货物抵达时部分受损。我们不得不对损害提出申诉。

d）I am looking forward to your due attention and proper solution on this matter.

我期待着你对这件事的关注和正确处理。

e）Although this letter will lead you to your inconvenience, I still want to complain about the use of computers.

尽管这封信可能会导致你的不便，但我还是想要抱怨电脑的使用问题。

f）The function of this product is quite different from that of the introduction.

这款产品的功能和介绍有很大的差别。

g）This product causes great trouble to my daily life.

这个产品对我的日常生活造成了极大的困扰。

h) We are sorry to inform you that the machines were badly damaged.

我们很遗憾地通知你这机器已经严重损坏。

i) We do hope that you'll take measures to solve the problem.

我们希望你会采取措施来解决这个问题。

j) We shall be glad if you will replace all phones as soon as possible.

如果你尽快将所有手机更换，我们将会很高兴。

范例 1 | 投诉商品错误（瑕疵，损毁）

Dear Sir,

We are writing to inform you that the furniture covered by our order No.624 arrived in such an unsatisfactory condition that we have to lodge a claim against you.

It was found upon examination that 15% of them are badly scratched, obviously due to the improper packing and transportation. Therefore, we cannot offer it for sale at the normal price and suggest that you make us an allowance of 20% on the invoiced cost. This is the amount by which we propose to reduce our selling price. If you cannot accept, I'm afraid we shall have to return them for replacement.

We hope you will immediately take this matter into your careful consideration and favor us with a prompt solution.

Yours sincerely,

Tom

尊敬的先生：

我们写信通知贵方，624号订单家具已收到，但货物状况令人很不满意，故我们不得不提出索赔。

经检查，我们发现有15%的货物有严重刮损现象。很明显，这是由于包装不当和运输途中所造成的。因此，我们无法以原价销售货物。建议贵方依照发票进价给予20%的折扣，这也是我们建议降低的销售额度。如果你方无法接受，我们将要求退货更换。

希望贵公司会立即慎重考虑，并马上惠告解决方案。

汤姆 谨上

邮件回复 *Reply*

Dear Tom,

We have for acknowledgement your letter dated Match 10 and are sorry to note your complaint respecting the furniture we sent to you. We can assure you, however, that the goods in question were in perfect order when they left here; hence, we are apparently not liable for the damage and would advise you to claim on the shipping company who should be responsible.

At any rate, we deeply regret to learn from you about this unfortunate incident and should it be necessary we shall be pleased to take the matter up on your behalf with the shipping company concerned.

Yours faithfully,

John Smith

亲爱的汤姆：

你方3月10日来函收悉。对你方所提出的家具索赔，我方深感遗憾。我方可以保证，该批次货物离开此地时状况完好。因此，我方不能对货物损坏负责，我们建议你方向装运公司提出索赔，因为他们应对此事负责。

无论如何，发生这种不幸之事确实令人感到遗憾。如有必要，我们愿代你方与装运公司洽谈此事。

约翰·史密斯 谨上

读书笔记

范例 2 | 投诉订单取消

Dear Sirs,

We are writing to complain about your cancelling our order No.9701 of 10,000 wedding gowns we placed with you on March 29, 2020.

We must point out that this cancellation brought us great inconvenience. Christmas is coming around, so us the peak season for wedding gowns. However, our present stock is nearly exhausted, which makes us unable to meet customers' demands, who, consequently, will place their orders elsewhere. We will suffer a great loss because of your cancellation.

We hope you will understand our situation and work out a satisfactory solution to this matter; otherwise we will feel obliged to apply for arbitration.

Yours sincerely,
Zhou Liyan
BBC Company

尊敬的先生：

我们写这封信是要投诉你方取消了我方2020年3月29日所下的10000件结婚礼服的订单，订单编号为9701。

我们必须指出，你们的行为给我们造成了极大的不便。圣诞节即将到来，随之而来的是结婚礼服的销售旺季。然而，我们目前的库存几乎告罄，将不能满足我们客户的需求；他们将会通过别的商家订货。由于你方不执行我方订单我方将承受巨大损失。

我们希望你们了解我们的处境，提出令人满意的解决方案；否则我们将不得不申请仲裁。

BBC公司
周立言 谨上

读书笔记

邮件回复 *Reply*

Dear Mr. Zhou,

We acknowledge with regret receipt of your letter dated March 29, 2019, complaining the cancellation of your order. We are very sorry for the inconvenience we have caused you.

As we have stated in the previous letter, we are now in full load, and unable to accept more orders. We herewith recommend another manufacturer in our area, which is specialized in garments. ACG Company also enjoys good reputation at home and abroad, and what's more, they have many factories distributed all over the country. We have introduced your company to them, and they are willing to accept your order and ensure you will not miss the peak season.

For further discussion, you can contact them at 027-89661567.

We again apologize for not being able to execute your order and the trouble it brought to you.

Yours sincerely,

Zhang Jin

HUG Company

亲爱的周先生：

我们很遗憾收到你方2019年3月29日有关取消你方订单的投诉信。我们对我方给你方造成的不便表示道歉。

正如我们上一封信所申明的那样，我们的生产已经满负荷，不可能再接受更多的订单了。我们因此向你方推荐本地的另一家专业服装生产商。ACG公司也是一家在国内外享有良好声誉的公司，而且他们在全国各地都设有工厂。我们已经把你们介绍给他们，他们愿意接受你们的订单，并且能够保证你们不会错过销售旺季。

你们可以拨打027—89661567与他们详谈。

我们再次对于我们未能执行你方订单及其给你方带来的麻烦表示道歉。

HUG公司

张金 敬上

范例 3 | 投诉售价金额错误

Dear Sir,

When your sales representative Mr. Liu called on me last month, he told me that you were offering a special price of ￥1,280 on the Wizard refrigerator this month. I ordered 10, figuring the total amount of the order at ￥12,800. However, the invoice that accompanied the shipment showed the amount due as ￥13,500. It is apparent that I was charged the regular price of ￥1350 instead of the lower price I was promised.

In enclosing a check for ￥12,800 in payment of the order. If this is not the case, I would like your permission to return the 10 refrigerators to you at your expense.

Yours sincerely,

Yang Yang

尊敬的先生：

当贵方销售代表刘先生上个月拜访我时，告知这个月奇术冰箱将以每台1280元的价格销售。我订购了10台，应付12800元。然而，随货所收的发票显示总价是13500元。显然，贵方的销售价仍为1350元，而非所许诺的低廉价格。

随函附上一张12800元的支票。如果情况不是这样的话，请允许我退回10台冰箱，所需费用由贵方支付。

杨扬 敬上

邮件回复 Reply

Dear Sir,

Thank you for your letter referring to the amount of your order.

We have investigated the matter and find that we did make a mistake. The 10 refrigerators will be sold still at the special price of ￥1,280.

We apologize for the mistake we made and the inconvenience. I hope it won't affect our cooperation.

Yours faithfully,

Jenny Chen

尊敬的先生：

多谢您有关订单金额来信。

经过我们的查证，我们的确在货款上有所失误。这10台冰箱我们还是以1280元的特价卖给您。

因此失误以及给您带来的不便，本公司深表歉意。希望这次的失误不会影响双方公司今后的合作。

陈詹尼 敬上

范例 4 | 投诉未开具发票

Dear Sirs,

We thank you for your prompt delivery of the order No.4212 on last Friday, March 12th, 2020.

Everything is satisfactory except that you seemed to forget to provide us the invoice for this order. We believe this must be due to your occasional negligence.

We will appreciate it if you can send it to us as soon as possible.

Yours sincerely,

Zhao Jiang

BBC Company

尊敬的先生：

我方很感谢你方将我方2020年3月12日即上周五所下的4212号订单货物迅速交付。

这次交易一切都令人满意，除了一点：你们似乎忘记了开具发票。我们相信这是由于你们偶然的疏忽所致。

如果你方能够尽快将发票寄送给我方，我方将不胜感激。

BBC公司

赵江 谨上

邮件回复 Reply

Dear Mr. Zhao,

We have received you letter of March 24th, 2020, complaining that you did not get the invoice for your order. We apologize for the trouble our negligence has caused to you.

Enclosed please find the invoice with the value of US $300,000.

Yours faithfully,

Zhou Bo

PPT Company

亲爱的赵先生：

我们收到了你方2020年3月24日的来信，投诉你方没有收到此次订单的发票。我方为由于我们的疏忽给你方带来的不便表示歉意。

附件请查收金额为300000美元的发票一份。

PPT公司

周波 敬上

读书笔记

范例 5 | 投诉商家取消订单

Dear Sirs,

We are writing to complain about your cancellation of order No. 3919.

We began to arrange production upon receiving your order and this batch of goods were made to your specifications. Your can cellation will cause great loss to our company, since it is impossible for us to sell the products to others.

We hope you can understand our situation and withdraw your cancellation; otherwise we will be obliged to apply for arbitration.

Yours sincerely,

Zhou Bo

UGB Company

尊敬的先生：

我写这封信是就你方撤销编号为3919订单一事进行投诉。

我们一接到你方的订单就开始组织生产，而且这批货物时根据你方的具体标准定制的。定制品不可能销售给别家厂商，因此你方取消订单势必会造成我公司的重大损失。

我们希望你方能够体谅我们的处境，收回撤销申请；否则我们不得不申请仲裁。

UGB公司

周波 敬上

邮件回复 *Reply*

Dear Mr. Zhou,

We are sorry for your letter of March 14th.

It was agreed that the order should be delivered no later than March 10th, but we did not receive them until March 11th. We had to execute our right according to the contract.

We hope you will comply with our cancellation at your earliest convenience.

Yours sincerely,

Zhang Hang

BEC Company

亲爱的周先生：

我们收到你方3月14日的来信，感觉非常遗憾。

我们先前约定的交货日期最晚为3月10日，但我们直到11日都没有收到货物。我们只能依照合同行使我们的权利。

我们希望你方能够尽早执行我们的订单取消申请。

BEC公司

张航 敬上

范例 6 | 投诉违反合约

Dear Sir,

We are writing to complain about your unilateral breach of our contract.

We ordered 50 Baier refrigerators with you on March 20, 2020 and we received the shipment yesterday. However, we found the refrigerators were not like the sample you showed to our purchasing staff. We ordered model CF1234 instead of CD1445. We phoned to your sales representatives for an explanation. He told us CF1234 was out of stock and they sent us CD1445 instead. We are quite unsatisfactory with this since CD1445 is an old model bearing a lot of shortcomings.

Our contract stipulated the exact model and your behavior was apparently against the item. We reserve the right to cancel the order and ask for full refund of the purchase price if you can not deliver us the right model. We will send you back those refrigerators we don't want to your expense.

Yours sincerely,

Zhang Qin

尊敬的先生：

我们写这封信是要投诉你方单方面违反合约。

我方于2020年3月20号向你方订购了50台拜尔电冰箱。昨日我们收到货物，却发现货物与你方之前向我方采购人员展示的样品不符。我们订购的型号是CF1234而非CD1445。我们电话联系了你们的销售代表要求做出解释。他告诉我们由于CF1234缺货，所以给我送来CD1445。我们对此表示非常不满，我们知道CD1445不仅型号老旧而且存在许多弱点。

我们签订的合同明确规定了产品型号，你方的行为显然违背了相关条款。如果你们不给我送来正确的型号，我们有权取消订单并要求全额退还购机款。我们将会把这批我们不愿接受的冰箱送还你方，运费由你方承担。

张勤 敬上

邮件回复 Reply

Dear Ms. Zhang,

We received with regret your letter of March 29, complaining the wrong model of the refrigerators.

We have studied your case, checking the contract and the shipping document and calling the sales representative who was responsible for your order. We have to admit we did deliver the wrong model. We attend our sincere apology for the trouble and inconvenience we have caused you.

We will arrange to ship the model you ordered as soon as possible.

Yours sincerely,

Tang Na

亲爱的张女士：

我们收到你方3月29日关于电冰箱型号错误的投诉，深表遗憾。

我们已经对这一问题进行了调查，核对了合同及装运单，并且电话联系了负责你方此次订单的销售代表。我们不得不承认我们投递的型号确实有误。我们对给你方造成的麻烦与不便表示诚恳的道歉。

我们将会尽快安排运送你们订购的型号。

唐纳 敬上

读书笔记

范例 7 | 投诉交货延期

Dear Sirs,

In your letter of March 15, which confirmed that our shipment of casual suits order No. 3011 had been placed on board Liberty; you stated that we could expect delivery of the merchandise no later than March 23.

However, as of now, we have not yet received the shipment. It is very important that we have the shipment by no later than the end of this month.

If you cannot assure us that the delivery problem will be solved, we are afraid that we will have no choice but to find another supplier.

We would be grateful if you would check into what happened to the shipment.

Yours sincerely,

EDC Company

尊敬的先生：

贵方3月15日来信告知我们我方编号为3011的休闲套装订单已经装上了自由号。你方还说明我们能够在3月23日收到货物。

然而直到现在，我们还没有收到该批货品。我们务必要在本月底之前收到货物。

如果你们不能保证圆满解决送货问题，我们恐怕就没有别的选择只好联系别家供货商了。

如果你方能够查清装船问题，我方将不胜感激。

EDC公司 敬上

邮件回复 *Reply*

Dear Sir or Madam:

We have received your letter of March 27, and apologize for the delay of your shipment.

We have checked with the shipping company, knowing that the unexpected delay was due to the vessel contracted to ship your order suddenly needed repairs.

We are glad, however, your shipment will arrive next Monday, and it will not miss the peak season.

Yours sincerely,

PPO Company

亲爱的先生/女士：

我们收到了你方3月27日的来信，并为我方未能及时交货道歉。

通过询问船运公司，得知此次意外延期是由于合约规定中为你运货的船只需要紧急维修。

我们很高兴地通知你方，你们的货物将于下周一到达，不会错过销售旺季。

PPO公司 敬上

范例 8 | 投诉配送地点错误

Dear Sir,

We are writing to complain about your distribution error.

We placed the order No.9545 with you on March 10, 2020 and our contract stipulated that the consignment should be delivered to Yangluo Port, Wuhan before the date of March 25, 2020. However, we were informed that our shipment arrived in Wuhan Port yesterday. It is obvious that you have made a mistake.

We would appreciate it if you can contact with the shipping company to change the delivery location. We hope to receive the shipment as soon as possible so that we will not miss the peak season.

Yours sincerely,

An Fang

DOC Company

尊敬的先生：

我们写这封信是要对你方的配送地址错误进行投诉。

我方于2020年3月10日向你方下了编号为9545的订单，合同标明这批货物须于2020年3月25日前运达武汉阳逻港。然而，我们昨日收到通知货物抵达武汉港。很显然你方犯了一个错误。

如果你方能够与船运公司取得联系，变更送货地址，我们将不胜感激。我们希望尽快收到货品，以赶上销售旺季。

DOC公司

安芳 谨上

邮件回复 *Reply*

Dear Ms. An,

We have contacted with the shipping company and the destination has been changed into Yangluo Port. You can expect to receive the good before the end of month.

We hope you can accept our apology with the same sincerity in which it is made.

Yours sincerely,

Zhang Hua

BBC Company

亲爱的安女士：

我们已经与船运公司取得联系，已将送货地址变更为阳逻港。你们应该能在本月底收到货物。

我们诚恳地向你们表示道歉，希望你们以同样的诚挚接受我们的道歉。

BBC公司

张华 敬上

范例 9 | 投诉售后服务不佳

Dear Sir,

We are writing to complain about your poor after sale service.

Our company brought a brand new Peugeot car from you two months ago. Only half a month after we picked it up, the car broke down and caused great inconvenience to our manager.

Last week, a rear panel fell off on a trip to the country, which your dealer in Wuhan refused to replace for free, claiming that it was the driver's fault for driving over rough roads. We paid for the replacement but found it unsatisfactory because it was an old one with obvious scratches.

We are a loyal customer of your company and have brought five cars from you. Our previous purchases were quite satisfactory and we hope you will deal with our complaint properly this time; otherwise we will have to buy cars from other manufacturers in the future.

Yours sincerely,

Zhang Jin

尊敬的先生：

我们写这封信是要就你们欠佳的售后服务进行投诉。

我们公司两个月前从贵公司购买了一辆全新的标致汽车。仅在我们提货半个月后，汽车就发生了故障，给我们的经理造成了很大的麻烦。

上周，在开往郊区的途中，汽车的后面板掉下来了。你们的武汉地区经销商坚称我们的司机不应该将车开到崎岖不平的路上，拒绝为我们免费更换新面板。我们只好付费维修，但却发现更换的面板不能令人满意，因为这是一块旧面板且带有明显的划痕。

我们是贵公司忠实的消费者，已经从贵公司购买了5辆汽车。之前的购买经历都十分令人满意，我们希望这次你们能恰当处理我们的投诉。否则以后我们将不得不从别处购买汽车。

张金 谨上

邮件回复 Reply

Dear Mr. Zhang,

We acknowledge with regret receipt of your complaint about our after sale service. We are sorry for the inconvenience you experienced.

We have checked with our dealer in Wuhan, who sent us a copy of the maintenance certificate for your car. According to the document, they have replaced your broken rear panel with a brand new one.

However, we have decided to repair those scratches for you without charge due to good faith. You can drive the car to the dealer this Saturday morning or you can contact them at 027-89223714 for an appointment if you are unavailable at that time.

Yours sincerely,

Zhang Liu

亲爱的张先生：

我们很遗憾收到您关于我们售后服务的投诉信。我们对给您带来的不便表示道歉。

我们与我们武汉的经销商进行了确认，他们寄来了一份您汽车的维修证明。该文件表明，他们给您更换了一块全新的后面板以代替您破损的旧面板。

但是，为了表达我们的诚意，我们还是决定为您免费修复那些划痕。您可于本周六上午将车开到经销商处，如果时间不便您可以拨打027—89223714与他们另行预约。

张柳 敬上

读书笔记

范例 10 | 投诉商品质量问题

Dear Sirs,

We are very sorry to inform you that the suits delivered to us yesterday are in no way up to the agreed specification.

We enclose one copy of inspection certificate No.1234 from a local surveyor, which proves that the above-mentioned goods are inferior in quality. Since the consignment falls short of the requirements of our customers entirely, we have to cancel our order and claim for inspection charges of US $ 3,500.

This is the first transaction between us and we hope you will promptly remedy it. Once the claim is settled, we will dispatch the goods back to you but all the charges should be for your account.

Truly yours,
Zhao Hua
BBT Company

尊敬的先生：

我方很遗憾地通知你方，我方昨天收到的套装根本达不到约定的标准。

我方随信寄上一份由本地检验人员出具的编号为1234的检验证明书。该证明书表明上述货品质量低劣。由于这批货物完全达不到我方消费者的要求，我方只好取消订单，并向你方索赔3500美元的检查费用。

这是我们之间的第一次交易，我方希望你方能够采取快速的补救措施。一旦索赔费用交付，我方就会将货物发还给你方，但所有费用必须由你方承担。

BBT公司
赵华 谨上

邮件回复 *Reply*

Dear Mr. Zhao,

Upon receiving your complaint regarding the quality of the consignment, we are very sorry that this batch of products failed to meet your requirements. After double checking the specified items in the contract and a sample of the goods we sent to you, we are obliged to admit the reasonability of your complaint. We are now discussing about this matter and trying to provide a satisfactory solution.

We apologize for the inconvenience we brought to you.

Yours sincerely,
Zhou Liyan
BOG Company

尊敬的赵先生：

收到你方关于货物质量的投诉，我方非常抱歉这批货品未能达到你方的要求。通过再次核对合同上的具体条款，并且比照该批货物的样品，我方不得不承认你方投诉是合理的。我方正在就此问题进行讨论，并尽可能提供一个满意的解决方案。

我方对给你方带来的不便表示道歉。

BOG公司
周立言 敬上

Unit 13 理赔信

(1) 如何写理赔信

理赔信是生意上的协商和赔偿事宜洽谈的一种书面方式。内容包括以下几个方面：

a）理赔信要写明写信人的姓名、写信日期和收信人的姓名或单位。

b）文章称呼要正规，如果知道对方姓名，要有尊称。

c）首先要对自己已收到的要求表示感谢，用词客气友善。然后表明已经对提出的问题进行了研究和调查以及得到的结果并说明原因。最后表明是否进行赔偿。

d）结尾处写出如果客户对此处理有异议，欢迎来函商洽，希望继续保持良好的合作等。

e）最后写上“特此复函，谢谢”和一些祝福语。

(2) 实用例句

a）Your letter has been received, thank you very much.

贵公司的来信已收悉，十分感谢。

b）Our company will follow and investigate the matter.

我公司就此事进行跟踪调查。

c）Our company has an honest and reliable reputation.

本公司有着诚实可靠的信誉。

d）Therefore, I will not accept the claims of non-quality problems.

因此，我公司将不接受非质量问题的理赔。

e）If the handling of the matter is in doubt, welcome the continuation of the letter to negotiate.

若对此事的处理还存在异议，欢迎继续来函商洽。

f）Achieving higher levels of product quality and customer satisfaction is always the purposes of our company.

追求更高水平的产品质量和客户满意度是我公司永远的宗旨。

g) Hope to continue to maintain sound cooperative relations with your company.

希望继续与贵公司保持良好合作关系。

h) We will make you a compensation of $750 by the way of T/T to settle your claim.

我们将电汇750美元给你们用于赔偿。

i) We are always pleased to hear from a valued customer.

我们很乐意听取有价值的客户的意见。

j) I am very sorry you did not receive the goods you wanted.

对于您没有收到想要的货物我表示抱歉。

范例 1 | 航班延误的理赔

Dear sir or madam,

I am writing in regards to the sudden and unannounced cancellation of my reserved flight for July 24 from Denver to Detroit (Confirmation Number: 772WB7; Airline Ticket Number: 0122150942247). Nobody called or emailed me to tell me that this flight was cancelled. I missed an important business meeting with my client as a result. Yes, I was put on a later flight, but imagine my outrage and fury when I walked into the empty conference room three hours behind the scheduled meeting!

I want an explanation and compensation for the inconvenience. And calling it "inconvenience" is putting it mildly.

John

亲爱的先生/女士：

我写这封信是为突然而没有通知的取消了7月24日从丹佛到底特律的航班。这次航班的确认号是772WB7，机票号是0122150942247。没有人打电话或者发邮件告诉我航班已经取消了。我因此错过了和我的顾客的一个重要会议。虽然我乘坐下一班飞机去了，但当我走进会议室时，会议已经结束三个小时了，你们可以想象出我当时有多生气。

我需要你们为我造成的不便给一个解释。用“不便”一词已经是很客气了。

约翰

邮件回复 *Reply*

Dear John,

Thank you for your email regarding the cancellation of flight 1226 which caused you to miss a meeting on July 24. On behalf of our airline, I sincerely apologize for that you did not give proper notice of the cancelled flight.

I understand the frustration you experienced when your plans were disrupted due to the cancellation of our flight for crew reasons. I am very sorry your travel was adversely affected.

Although I am not able to issue a refund on flown travel, I have added 7,500 World Perks bonus miles to your account. You may visit our website to verify. Please allow three business days for miles to appear.

Mr. John, please know that we work very hard to operate every flight as scheduled. Given the opportunity of serving you in the future, I am confident we will meet your expectations.

Sincerely,

Mr. White

亲爱的约翰：

很感谢你写信来反映因为取消1226航班使你错过了在7月24日的会议的事。我代表公司为未能及时通知你航班取消表示道歉。

我能够理解你因航班取消计划被打乱而带来的困境。很抱歉你的旅行计划被我们耽搁了。

我不能给你飞行旅行退款，但我在您的账户加入了7500里程奖励。希望你在我们的网站上确认。这将在三个工作日内到达。

我们已经很努力地安排每个航班。希望以后能够为你服务。我相信到时候一定会满足你的要求。

怀特先生

范例 2 | 行李丢失的理赔

Dear Sir or Madam,

This law firm represents passenger Mr. Wu regarding a missing luggage claim. Enclosed please find a notarized copy of the power of attorney as signed by Mr. Wu.

Mr. Wu was a passenger in your flight (UA982) from New York City to Beijing on April 16, 2019. On arriving at Beijing International Airport, Mr. Wu's luggage, being an olive-green plastic suitcase by the size of approximately 85 cm × 95 cm × 35 cm, was lost. Mr. Wu duly registered the loss with the airport authority and the local service counter of your airlines. Enclosed please find a copy of the Loss Claim Receipt as registered with and issued by your service counter representative.

After more than one month, you have not yet found Mr. Wu's suitcase. Enclosed please find a list containing items in the suitcase,including an IBM laptop computer valued at USD $1,299.00 plus tax, a Sony digital camera priced at USD 399.00 plus tax, clothing and various personal items valued at roughly $2,000.00. The total is $3,898.00. Please pay this amount payable to Mr. Wu.

Please process this claim expeditiously and keep us informed accordingly.

Very truly yours,

Law Offices of Lee

亲爱的先生 / 女士：

本法律事务所代表吴先生来对一只丢失的行李进行理赔。附件中有吴先生的委托书。

吴先生乘坐UA982航班于2019年4月16日从纽约到北京。在到达北京后，吴先生的一只大约为85cm × 95cm × 35cm的橄榄绿的行李箱不见了。吴先生和机场相关人员进行了登记。在附件中有一份相关信息的复印件。

在一个月之后，你们还是没有找到吴先生的箱子。附件中有一份箱子中物品的清单。这份清单包括IBM电脑（价值1299美元加税）、索尼数码相机（价值399美元加税）、衣物和一些私人物品价值2000美元。总的价值是3898美元。请向吴先生支付这些钱。

请尽快处理此要求，并通知我们。

Lee律师事务所

邮件回复 *Reply*

Dear Mr. Li,

We have received your requirement claim. We will do as what you have asked as soon as possible. I am sorry that Mr. Wu's suitcase was lost on our plane. We have tried our best to find it. But we have not found it now. We have contacted Mr. Wu, and negotiated with him on related things. After we have handled this thing, we will inform you.

Wish you work successfully!

Yours sincerely

Mr. Black

亲爱的李先生：

我们已经收到你的理赔要求。我们会很快处理这些要求的。很遗憾，吴先生的行李箱是在乘坐我们公司的航班时丢失的。我们已经尽我们全力去寻找，但还是没有找到。我们已经和吴先生取得联系，并就相关问题进行协商。等我们处理完后，会通知你们相关信息。

祝工作顺利！

布莱克

读书笔记

范例 3 | 货品瑕疵的理赔

Dear Customer,

Hello!

Your customer's letter of May 10th has been received. The letter referred to the basketball shoes with fracture in my shop. We have investigated the matter and found that all the shoes of this shipment have the same problem. With the spirit of honest and reliable reputation of such quality problems, We decided to give you a full refund or a group of new stock for replacing. You are welcomed for the continuation of the letter with valuable advice.

Achieving higher levels of product quality and customer satisfaction is always our purposes.

Hereby reply, thank you!

Tom

May 21th, 2020

尊敬的客户：

您好！

您5月10日的来信已收悉。信中提到我店的篮球鞋鞋底断裂，我店就此事进行调查，发现这批货都有这种问题。本公司本着诚实可靠的信誉，对此种质量问题，决定给予您全额退款或者换一批新货。欢迎继续来函提出宝贵意见。

追求更高水平的产品质量和客户满意度是我公司永远的宗旨。

特此复函，谢谢！

汤姆

2020年5月21日

邮件回复 *Reply*

Dear Sir,

I have received your letter. I also know the approach of your shop. I chose a replacement. Hope to continue to maintain a good working relationship with your store.

Hereby reply, thank you!

Kate

May 23th, 2020

亲爱的先生：

你来信我已经收到。贵店提出的处理方法我也知道了。我选择换货。

希望继续与贵店保持良好的合作关系。

特此回复，谢谢！

凯特

2020年5月23日

范例 4 | 货品寄发错误的理赔

Dear Customer,

The tie with a plaid motif was sent today by Priority Mail to replace the tie you received with a stripe motif.

You know, one would think it would be impossible to make an error like this. You clearly specified in your order that the tie was to be put on in an important meeting. The stock number you supplied was correct. There was no reason for a ship up at this end, and I can't even guess how it happened.

I am much relieved, however, that you will have the right tie in time.

When you get around to it, would you please send the stripe one to me? I'll pay the postage.

Tom

September 11th, 2012

亲爱的顾客：

退换条纹领带的格子领带已于今天用快递发出。

你可能会认为这样的错误几乎是不可能的。在你的订单中你清楚的指明是在一个很重要的会议中要使用的。你的订单号码也是正确的。没有理由出现错误，我也无法想象这是如何发生的。

非常庆幸的事，你会及时地收到正确的领带。

当你收到领带时，请将条纹领带寄回好吗？我将承担邮费。

汤姆

2012年9月11日

邮件回复 *Reply*

Dear Tom,

Your letter and tie have been received. I am very satisfied with the new tie which was the one I ordered. I have delivered the stripe tie back to you and please pay for the postage when it arrives. Look forward to the next cooperation.

White

September 12th, 2012

亲爱的汤姆：

来信和领带都已经收到，新的领带我非常满意，正是我当时订的那款。条纹领带已经寄出，邮费将在收件时由您付。期待下次合作。

怀特

2012年9月12日

范例 5｜交货延迟的理赔

Dear Sir,

We have been doing business together for a long time and we value our relationship, we have been able to provide the kind of service we both want. The problem is that your purchasing department always changes orders after they have been placed. This has led to the goods been delivered late. According to the contract, we can't pay for your loss just for this. To solve the problem, I think you should tell us what you want in time. If you don't agree with this, you can put forward to your specific requirements.

Yours,

Tom

亲爱的先生：

我们已经合作了很长时间，我很珍视我们之间的关系，我们一直能提供双方满意的服务。问题是你方采购部门在拿货之后经常改变订单。这导致了货物交付延迟。根据合同，我们不能仅仅因为这个就进行赔付。为了解决这个问题，我认为你方应及时将要求告知我方。如果对此不满意，你可以告知你的具体要求。

汤姆

邮件回复 *Reply*

Dear Tom,

As I know, it was negligence of our purchasing department in this matter. The strict requirements have already been put forward and we will timely inform you next time. Wish a good cooperation in the future.

Yours,

Jimmy

亲爱的汤姆：

经过我的了解，我方采购部门在这件事情上确实存在疏忽。我已经对他们提出了严格的要求，下次会及时地告知你方。希望今后的合作愉快。

吉米

范例 6 | 商品数量错误的理赔

Dear Customer,

Immediately after we received your letter we dispatched two refrigerators which left for your city. They are expected to reach your center warehouse in 3 days.

Every individual product or service of our company is fully guaranteed, and we are glad to make this adjustment for you. Thank you for writing us so promptly.

The mistake occurred as a result of staff shortage during an unusually busy season. We forget to check on the quantity of goods. We wish to express our concern for the inconvenience we have caused you.

Thank you again for your cooperation.

Yours,

Jason

亲爱的顾客：

收到你的信，我们就立刻调拨了2台为你们城市预留的冰箱。三天内将会送达你们的中心仓库。

每一个我们提供的产品或者服务都是有着充分保证的，我们很乐意为你调整。感谢你如此迅速地给我们写信。

由于旺季人手短缺，所以导致了这个错误。员工忘了对货物数量进行核查。由此对你产生的不便，我们深表歉意。

再次感谢与我们的合作。

杰森

邮件回复 *Reply*

Dear Jason,

I have received the refrigerators. It's so fast, and I'm very satisfied with them. I understand your mistakes. The goods needed to be sent are too many recently after all. I hope it can be avoided next time.

Tommy

亲爱的杰森：

冰箱已收到，速度很快，货物很满意。对于你们的失误我表示理解，毕竟最近的货物确实多。希望下次能避免再次发生此类事件。

汤米

范例 7 | 货品重量短缺的理赔

Dear Hanson,

You will be enjoying new boxes of apples which we delivered to you yesterday. They will reach you no later than August 10. We received your letter in which you expressed that the apples are short in weight. We are sorry to learn that.

Our representative looked into the matter immediately in your city because we are always desirous of offering our customers the best apples.

Of course, we should realize that sometimes an incident such as this occurs and we are sending the apples you requested. We are sure that the newly delivered boxes will meet your satisfaction.

Please send back the original boxes of apples in time. If we can assist you in any way in the future, please let us know.

Yours,

Jim

亲爱的汉森：

你将会很满意我们昨天发送给你的新成箱的苹果。它们最晚于8月10日前到达。我们之前收到了您的来信，在来信中你表达苹果的重量不足，对此我们表示非常的遗憾。

我公司让您所在城市的代表立即调查了这一事件，因为我们希望提供给我们的客户最好的苹果。

当然，我们要认识到有时会有这样的事件发生。按照你的要求我们发送了新的苹果。我们确信，这一批发送的苹果会令您满意。

请及时寄回原箱苹果。如果以后我们有什么可以帮助的，请告诉我们。

吉姆

邮件回复 *Reply*

Dear Jim,

The shortage in weight of apples almost causes our customer complaints. Fortunately, your company brought the new boxes of apples in time. As our long-term cooperation relations, we don't pursue the incident. Wish our cooperation smooth.

Hansen

亲爱的吉姆：

这次苹果的重量不足，差点造成客户的投诉。幸好你们公司及时送来了新的苹果。鉴于我们长期的合作关系，这次事件我方不予以追究。愿以后合作顺利。

汉森

范例 8 | 货品缺损的索赔

Dear Jackson,

Thank you for your letter in which you lodged a claim for broken schoolbags. We will replace them with new ones.

We wish to express our deep regret at this incident. We took your case seriously, and have looked into the matter in detail. After checking three broken schoolbags you sent to us, we found that it was because the bags had been treated with much heat in the packing procedure.

We are most concerned to maintain our long-term trading relationship. Meanwhile, we have taken some corrective measures to prevent a repetition of the same mistake in the future.

We hope this matter will not affect our good relations in our future dealings.

Yours,

Ethan

亲爱的杰森：

非常感谢你来信提出的书包损坏的赔偿问题。我们将会为你更换新的书包。

对于这个事情，我们深表遗憾。我们对问题的细节进行了仔细的检查。在检查三个你寄来的破损的书包时，我们发现是由于在包装时受热过量所导致。

我们非常重视彼此之间长期的合作关系。同时我们采取了一些纠正措施，防止再次发生。

希望这个意外不会影响我们未来良好的伙伴关系。

伊森

邮件回复 *Reply*

Dear Ethan,

I am very satisfied that you find out the cause of this problem so fast, and send me new bags. Sincerity is the foundation of the cooperation of both sides. I am sure that we will have a cordial working relationship in the future.

Jason

亲爱的伊森：

能够这么快查出问题的原因，并且换了新的书包，我非常满意。诚意是双方合作的基础，我相信今后我们也一定会合作愉快。

杰森

Unit 14 道歉篇

（1）如何写致歉信

a）直截了当的开始道歉，说明道歉的原因。

b）如果由于不得已而犯的错，要适当地加以解释，但不要开脱自己的责任；如果确实是自己的疏忽，就应该诚恳地进行道歉，表明自己一定会改过。

c）说明自己打算如何补救自己的过错，提出补救措施和建议。

d）真心道歉，希望得到对方的谅解。

（2）实用例句

a）I am writing to apologize that I can not participate in your birthday party tonight.

我写这封信是为了向你道歉，我不能参加你今晚的生日派对了。

b）Please accept my apology for breaking your bike this afternoon.

今天下午我弄坏了你的自行车，请接受我的道歉。

c）I deeply regret that I dirtied your clothes this morning.

我很后悔今天早上弄脏了你的衣服。

d）I know my behavior is not inexcusable, and I am so sorry for...

我知道我的行为是不容辩解的，我很抱歉……

e）This is my fault to... I will do everything I can to make some compensation.

这是我的错，我将会做一切事情进行补偿。

f）I was so concentrated on my book and didn't see you in front of me. I am sorry to knock over your coffee and dirty your clothes. I am so sorry to embarrass you.

我看书太专注了，没有看见你站在我前面，于是打翻了你的咖啡，弄脏了你的衣服。我很抱歉让你尴尬。

g）You can call someone to fix that bike. And I will pay for the bill. Please call me at ×××. My name is ×××. I feel so sorry to do that, but I was not on purpose.

你可以叫人来修理，我会付账单。请打电话给我，我的电话是×××，名字是×××。我感到很抱歉，但是我不是故意的。

h）If it is convenient for you, please give me your clothes and I will wash it and then give it back to you. Please give me your number.

如果方便的话，请把你的衣服给我，我会洗干净送还给你。请告诉我你的号码。

i）Please accept my sincere apology for doing that.

请接受我真挚的歉意。

j）I know it bothered you a lot and I will not do this anymore.

我知道这样做打扰到你，我保证不会再发生这样的事情了。

范例 1｜商品问题（错误、瑕疵、损坏等）的道歉

Dear Mr. Wang,

We have received your letter of March 18, informing us that the sewing machines we shipped to you arrived in a damaged condition on account of imperfectness of our pack. We are very sorry for that.

We are convinced that the present damage was due to extraordinary circumstances under which they were transported to you. So we are not responsible for the damage, but as we think that it would not be fair to have you bear the loss alone, we suggest that the loss be divided between both of us, to which we hope you will agree.

Yours faithfully,

×××

尊敬的王先生：

贵方3月18号的来信已收悉，得知我方发过去的缝纫机由于不完善的包装有一定的损坏。对于这件事我们感到很抱歉。

我们相信产品是在运输的途中由于特殊情况损坏的。所以我方并没有责任，但我方认为让贵方单独承担损失是不公平的，我们建议可以共同承担这个损失，希望贵方能同意。

×××谨上

邮件回复 *Reply*

Dear Sir or Madam,

Thank you for your letter and your proposal.

That is so kind of you to suggest that the loss be divided between both of us. We are delighted to accept the suggestion.

We think we can find some time to discuss the details. If you decide the date and time, please inform us.

Wang Ming

敬启者：

感谢贵方的来信与建议。

贵方能与我方共同承担损失真是太好了。我们非常愿意接受这个建议。

我们认为要找个时间去讨论下细节。如果贵方决定好日期和时间，请回复我们。

王明

范例 2 | 订货失误的道歉

Dear Mr. Wang,

I am writing to inform you that we made mistakes in placing order No.1234 with you. We planned to order white shirt size L, but the results turned to be that we have booked white shirt size M. We hereby request a correction of the mistake. We are quite clear that this will cause you trouble, for which we extend our sincere apology.

We would appreciate it if this situation could be resolved.

We look forward to your reply.

Yours sincerely,

Li Ming

尊敬的王先生：

我写信是想告诉您我方在贵方所下的编号为1234的订单发生了错误。我们本来打算是要订白色、L型号的衬衫，但结果我们订了白色、M型号的衬衫。我们现在要求修订这一错误。我们知道此事会给贵公司带来麻烦，还请海涵。

如果问题得到解决我们将不胜感激。

期待您的回信。

李明 谨上

邮件回复 *Reply*

Dear Mr. Li,

We acknowledge your letter of April 12, requesting a size change of the shirts.

We are delighted to grant your request, since we have not begun to arrange shipment.

Enclosed please find the contract, and make the amendment accordingly and then send back to us. Thank you for your cooperation.

Yours sincerely,

Wang Jing

尊敬的李先生：

贵方4月12日要求更改衬衫型号的信件收悉。

由于我们还没有安排装船，我们很高兴答应你方的请求。

附件请查收合同一份，请作相应修改后寄还我方。

感谢您的合作。

王京 谨上

范例 3 | 交货延迟的道歉

Dear Mr. Wang,

Please accept our apology for not being able to delivery the goods on time.

We cooperated with two companies at the same time. Since the production load was big, our machine turned out to be faulty, but fortunately the problem was resolved very soon.

The above incident caused the delay in delivery, for which we extend our sincerest apology and we would like to give you a 2% discount to compensate you.

Yours sincerely,

Li Ming

尊敬的王先生：

请接受我们对贵公司交货延迟的道歉。

之前我们与两家公司同时合作。因为生产工作量大，导致我们的机器出了一些故障，但幸好问题很快就得到了解决。

上述原因造成的延迟交货，对此，深感抱歉，我们愿意给你2%的折扣，以弥补一些损失。

李明 谨上

邮件回复 Reply

Dear Mr. Li,

We are sorry to hear that the goods we ordered on April 10 have not been delivered so far. This shipment delay is inconveniencing us, as we are now in urgent need of these products.

We have contacted our clients, who rejected your proposal. In this case, we have to cancel the order.

We will appreciate it if you can understand our situation.

Yours sincerely,

Wang Jing

尊敬的李先生：

我们在4月10号订的货物还没到达，对此我们感到很遗憾。由于我方迫切需要这些货物，你方延迟交货让我方处境困难。

我们已经与我们的客户取得联系，他们拒绝了你方的提议。在这种情况下，我方只能取消订单了。

如你方能够理解我方的处境，我方当不胜感激。

王京 谨上

范例 4 | 忘开发票的道歉

Dear Madam,

We have received your letter of April 12, 2020, complaining no invoice attached with the lady shaver you brought from us. We have to confess that it was due to our negligence. We checked our sales record, which is in accordance with the information you provided and made out an invoice for the item.

We apologize sincerely for the trouble we brought to you.

Enclosed please find an invoice.

Yours sincerely,

Li Ming

尊敬的女士：

我们已经收到了您于2020年4月12日关于投诉您从我处购买的女用剃毛刀未开发票的来信。我们不得不承认这是由我们的疏忽所致。我们查对了销售记录，发现与您提供的信息一致，我们已经为该商品补开了发票。

我们为给您带来的麻烦表示道歉。

随信附上发票一份。

李明 谨上

邮件回复 *Reply*

Dear Mr. Li,

I am writing to acknowledge receipt of your letter of March 22, 2020 and enclosed invoice. Thank you for your prompt attention.

Yours faithfully,

Mary

亲爱的李先生：

您2020年3月22日的来信及所附的发票已经收到。感谢您的及时处理。

玛丽 敬上

范例 5 | 开错发票的道歉

Dear Ms. Wang,

Thank you for your mail of March 15, 2020 regarding the wrong amount in the invoice for your order. We were able to track down the error and have corrected the figure accordingly. We are enclosing the amended invoice.

You are a valued customer and we apologize for any inconvenience this mistake may have caused. If we may be of further assistance please contact us at your convenience.

Yours sincerely,

BBC Company

尊敬的王女士：

感谢你方2020年3月15日有关你方订单发票金额错误的来信。我方已经查究了错误，并就金额作了相应的更正。随信附上修改过的发票一份。

你们是我们的重要客户，我们为这一错误可能造成的任何不便表示道歉。如果你们需要进一步的协助，请随时联系我们。

BBC公司 敬上

邮件回复 Reply

Dear Sir or Madam,

We have received your letter of March 20, and the enclosed invoice. Thank you for your prompt attention to our request.

We have been delighted to cooperate with you and hope to establish a longstanding business partnership with you.

Yours sincerely,

Wang Rong

尊敬的先生 / 女士：

我方已经收到你方3月20日的来信及所附发票。感谢你方迅速关照我方的要求。

我们很高兴与你们合作，并且希望能与你们建立长期的贸易伙伴关系。

王荣 敬上

范例 6 | 贷款滞纳的道歉

Dear Mr. Huang,

This mail is to extend our sincere apology for the late payment of the loan from your company. We were supposed to make a payment of ￥100,000 with a 6% interest on it on the 7th of last month. Unfortunately, we have not been able to do so due to the financial crises, which resulted in the recent slow market and our dropping sales. However, we shall make the due payments in the coming month. The interest as well as the late payment fees of ￥5,000 would be paid along with the installment.

We sincerely thank you for all the cooperation and sympathy that you and your organization have extended.

Yours sincerely,

Zhang Jun

尊敬的黄先生：

我们借由此信为我方滞纳贷款向你方表示道歉。我们本应于上月7号偿清10万元的货款及6%的利息。但由于金融危机影响，市场疲软导致了我们的销售量下滑，我们未能偿付上述款项。但我们会在下月将其偿清贷款、利息及滞纳金5000元。

感谢您和贵公司给予我们的同情和合作。

张军 敬上

邮件回复 Reply

Dear Mr. Zhang,

We acknowledge receipt of your letter of March 23, 2011.

We understand your situation and are willing to grant your request. But we hope to receive your payment the next month on time.

Yours faithfully,

Huang Yang

尊敬的张先生：

我们收到了你方2011年3月23号的来信。

我方了解你方处境，并同意你方的请求。但是我们希望下月能够按时收到款项。

黄杨 敬上

范例 7 | 汇款延迟的道歉

Dear Sirs,

I have received your letter dated March 30, 2020.

I failed to pay on time because I was away on business trip, so I'm sorry for that.

Now enclosed please find a draft for $100, 000, receipt of which please acknowledge.

Tom Smith

尊敬的先生们：

我们已收到贵方2020年3月30日来函。

由于出差外地，我没能按时支付货款，深感抱歉。

现附上100000美元汇票。收到后请告知我方。

汤姆 · 史密斯 敬上

邮件回复 Reply

Dear Mr. Smith,

We acknowledge receipt of your letter dated April 6,2020 and the enclosed draft for $100, 000. Thank you for your cooperation.

Yours sincerely,

BBC Company

尊敬的史密斯先生：

我们收到了你方2020年4月6日的来信及寄送的100000美元汇票。感谢你方的合作。

BBC公司 谨上

范例 8 | 忘记取消订单的道歉

Dear Sir or Madam,

On March 23, 2020, I booked a room at your hotel where I was due to be staying on April 13, 2020 for 1 night (booking ref: RH/3140), as I planned to attend a meeting in your city. Unfortunately, I was informed the meeting was cancelled on April 5 and, what was worse, I forgot to cancel the reservation until yesterday when the receptionist at your hotel called me for the reason why I did not check in.

I am quite sorry for the trouble I have caused you. And I will give up the ￥50 deposit for your compensation.

Yours sincerely,

Li Qing

尊敬的先生/女士：

我于2020年3月23日在你们酒店预订了一间房，预备2020年4月13日入住一晚（订单编号：RH/3140），准备参加在你市举行的一个会议。但在4月5日我接到通知该会议取消了。更糟糕的是，我居然忘记了取消预约，直到昨天你们酒店的前台打来电话询问我为什么没有入住。

我很抱歉给你们造成了麻烦。我放弃50元的定金作为对你方的赔偿。

李清 敬上

邮件回复 *Reply*

Dear Ms. Li,

We acknowledge receipt of your letter of April 14, explaining the reason you did not check in on April 13. We are sorry for not being able to serve you, but please allow us to serve you next time when you come to our city.

Yours sincerely,

ABC Hotel

尊敬的李女士：

我们收到了您4月14日的来信，阐明您4月13日没能入住我店的原因。我们为没能为您提供服务表示遗憾，但是下次您到我市来的时候请让我们为您服务。

ABC酒店 敬上

范例 9 | 延迟出具收据的道歉

Dear Ms. Green, After reading your letter of March 13, 2020, I can thoroughly understand your standpoint of making such a complaint. While it would be easy to place the blame on our computer, this poor fellow has received enough abuse since joining our firm. After all, he only follows the orders that are given to him. Therefore, please accept my apology for the delay in providing the invoice for your order No.1234. Our bookkeeping department has been instructed to make an invoice for you at once, which you should be receiving within a few days. I am grateful that your letter was brought to my attention and I appreciate your perseverance in settling this matter. Once again, I am very sorry for the inconvenience this has caused you. Yours sincerely, ABC Company	尊敬的格林女士： 贵方2020年3月13日的来函收悉，我能理解您投诉的立场。 我们本来可以很容易地归罪于我们的电脑，但是它自加入我们公司就承受了太多的责难。毕竟他也只是按指令行事。因此，请接受我们对与你方编号为1234的订单延迟出具收据的道歉。 我们的财务部门收到通知后立即给你方开具发票，你们应该可以在几天内收到。 我感谢您来信提醒我们，并赞赏您在此问题上执着的精神。 我再次对给您带来的不便表示抱歉。 ABC公司 敬上

邮件回复 *Reply*

Dear Sir or Madam, We acknowledge your letter of March 16, 2020 and we thank you for your prompt attention to our request. We will be willing to keep a cooperative business relationship with you. Yours sincerely, Ella Green	尊敬的先生/女士： 我们收到贵方2020年3月16日的来函，感谢你方对我方请求的迅速回应。我们愿意与你方保持合作贸易关系。 艾拉·格林 敬上

范例 10 | 商品目录更正的道歉

Dear Christina,

We have acknowledged your letter dated April 5 and are sorry to note your complaint about the wrong items in the catalogue.

Normally we are careful about this. The accident was due to our negligence. We extend our apologies for the inconvenience and loss this incidence has caused you, but we assure you that we will change the right item for the rest goods and make compensation to you because of the different price caused by the wrong price items.

Since we value your business, we would like to offer you a favorable discount of your next order with us.

We look forward to receiving your further orders and assure you similar errors will not occur again.

Yours faithfully,

John Smith

亲爱的克里斯蒂娜：

我们收到您4月5日寄来的信。对给您造成的麻烦，我们深表遗憾。

一般情况下，我们对于收据发送问题极为谨慎，此次纯属疏忽。我们对此事给您造成的不便和损失深感抱歉，但我们向您保证，对于余下商品，我们会予以更正，并且由于商品目录问题所引起的差价而让您遭受的损失我们会给予赔偿。

我们很重视与贵公司的合作，因此下次贵公司订购时我们将会提供优惠的折扣。

希望还能接到贵公司的订单，我们保证今后会注意让此类事情不再发生。

约翰 · 史密斯 谨上

邮件回复 *Reply*

Dear Smith,

We have acknowledged your reply about our complaint. Thank you for your prompt attention but we are afraid we can not accept the disposal. We are requesting a 15% of the amount of the order to compensate our loss.

Yours faithfully,

Christina

亲爱的史密斯：

你方针对我方投诉的回函收悉。感谢你方的及时回复，但是恐怕我们不能接受你方的处理方式。我们要求以货款的15%作为赔偿，弥补我方损失。

克里斯蒂娜敬上

范例 11 | 汇款金额不足的道歉

Dear Sirs,

We have received your mail of April 11, 2020, complaining that our remittance was not sufficient. We have checked it with our accountant and realized that we did make a mistake. We apologize for the inconvenience it has caused you.

We have sent you the draft for $100, 000 and we are enclosing another one for $ 5, 000. Please acknowledge receipt of it.

Yours faithfully,

Tom Smith

尊敬的先生们：

我们收到了你方2020年4月11日关于投诉我方汇款金额不足的邮件。经与我公司会计核查，我们意识到犯了错误。我们为给你方带来的麻烦表示道歉。

我们已经寄送了一份100000美元汇票，现在附上另一份5000美元汇票。收到后请通知我方。

汤姆·史密斯 敬上

邮件回复 *Reply*

Dear Mr. Smith,

We acknowledge receipt of your letter dated April 16, 2020 and the enclosed draft for $5, 000. Thank you again for your cooperation.

Yours sincerely,

BBC Company

尊敬的史密斯先生：

我们收到了你方2020年4月16日的来信及寄送的5000美元汇票。再次感谢你方合作。

BBC公司 谨上

范例 12｜意外违反合同的道歉

Dear Sir or Madam,

I am very regretful to hear that the quantity of the shipment wasn't in line with that stipulated in the contract.

We have studied the investigation report you sent to us and checked with the clerk who was responsible for your order, and we have to confess that due to our negligence we have made the mistake and it is against our contract. We are now arranging shipment for the rest of the consignment and we will inform you of the delivery date when it has been settled.

We extend our sincere apologies for any inconvenience you have experienced.

Yours sincerely,

Li Hua

尊敬的先生 / 女士：

对于你方所投诉产品的数量与合同上的不一致的问题，我们深表遗憾。

我们已经研究过你方给我方寄送的调查报告，经与我们的办事员核对，我们必须承认由于我们的疏忽，我们发生了错误，并违反了合同。我们正在安排其他货物的装船事宜，并且一旦到货时间确定，我方就会通知你方。

我们为给你方带来的不便表示道歉。

李华 谨上

邮件回复 *Reply*

Dear Ms. Li,

Thank you for your reply. We appreciate your disposal regarding this incident.

We would like to establish a long business relationship with you, since we can see you are a responsible partner through this incident.

Yours faithfully,

× × ×

亲爱的李女士：

感谢你的来信。我们很欣赏贵方在这件事上的态度。

我们愿意与贵公司建立长期的合作关系，因为从这件事我们认识到贵公司是有责任的合作伙伴。

× × × 谨上

范例 13 | 因爽约道歉

Dear Daisy,

I would like to express my apology for missing our 14 o'clock appointment.

A small accident happened to me when I was on my way to school. I am going to come over to your apartment the day after tomorrow — Monday, April4, at 2 p.m. If it is convenient for you, I will check my email tomorrow to make sure whether you have left a note for me. Otherwise, I will see you at 2 p.m., Monday afternoon.

I am very sorry for that again.

Best wishes,

Cathy

亲爱的黛西：

未能前去出席我们之间14点钟的约会，我感到非常抱歉。

我在去学校的路上发生了一个小意外。如果你没有别的安排，我将于后天，也就是4月14日（周一）下午两点去你的公寓拜访。我明天会检查邮箱查看是否有你的留言回复，如果没有，周一下午两点钟我将准时拜会你。

再次向你表示歉意！

祝好！

凯西

邮件回复 *Reply*

Dear Cathy,

I've got your message. I'm sorry you couldn't attend the meeting. Though I'd like to have a word with you, we have to chat next time because of the incident. I hope you don't have any trouble about it. I'll be home Monday afternoon, and welcome you to visit me.

Best wishes,

Daisy

亲爱的凯西：

我已经收到你的留言，很遗憾你不能出席我们之间的约会。虽然很想和你聊聊天，但是既然你有事就改下次了，希望你没有遇到什么麻烦的事才好。另外我周一下午会在家里，欢迎你的拜访。我随时恭候。

祝好！

黛西

范例 14 | 因缺席道歉

Dear Tom,

I'm really sorry for not catching up for your business review meeting this afternoon.

My flight was supposed to arrive at Dalian Zhoushuizi International Airport at 10:00. Unfortunately, the airport was closed because of an unexpected heavy fog, and my aircraft was forced to land on later than scheduled. This made it impossible for me to attend your meeting on time.

I have asked my secretary to prepare and send the meeting summary to my mailbox. I will circulate my input as soon as I review the summary.

Yours sincerely,

Davis

亲爱的汤姆：

未能出席今天下午举行的业务报告会，我感到十分抱歉。

我的航班原计划今天上午10点抵达大连周水子国际机场，可是不凑巧，由于大雾意外出现，大连周水子国际机场被迫关闭，我的飞机也因此晚点，这导致我不能按时参加会议。

我已吩咐秘书将本次会议的纪要整理好发送到我的电子邮箱，待我审阅后，就会将我的批注意见发送给所有与会者。

戴维斯

邮件回复 *Reply*

Dear Davis,

I am very sorry that you missed the meeting in the afternoon. Because you are the authority in this field. Your absence made the meeting cast into shade. However the meeting has made some important achievements on many important consensuses. You can have a look at the records of the meeting. Please be careful in the travel.

Yours,

Tom

亲爱的戴维斯：

对于今天下午您未能出席业务报告会，我感到很遗憾。因为您在这个行业的卓越成就，您的缺席令报告会逊色不少。不过大会也取得重要成就，达成许多重要共识，这一切您可以参考会议记录，请您注意旅途安全。

汤姆

范例 15 | 因造成损失道歉

Dear John,

Jack has explained to us the incident of your window broken by his football this morning. On knowing this, the first thing that I did was to order a new window on Taobao website and take down your address. They promised to send you a new window tomorrow and will be responsible for installation. Of course, the bill will be sent to me.

We are sincerely sorry that the accident occurred, and I know that all the boys will be more careful in the future.

Very sincerely yours,

Ruby

亲爱的约翰：

杰克告诉了我一个意外事故。今早他的足球打碎了你家的窗户。得知此事后，我就立即从淘宝网上订购了一扇新窗户，并且记下了你的地址。他们说明天会给你送一扇新窗户，并且负责安装，账单当然由我支付。

发生这样的事情我很抱歉，我想这些小男孩们今后会多小心。

露比

邮件回复 *Reply*

Dear Ruby,

I have received your messages. I've found the broken window yesterday. Little Jack has admitted his mistake gravely and has already explained it to me. I wish you not to punish the child. I was going to order a piece of glass. Since you have already bought one, I have to cancel the order.

Yours,

Jone

亲爱的露比：

你的邮件已经收到。我昨天已经发现窗户破碎的事，小杰克勇于承认自己的错误并已经向我说明，希望你不要责罚孩子，教育就行。我本来准备自己重新安装一块玻璃，既然你已经预定，就麻烦你了。

约翰

范例16 | 因失礼道歉

Dear Eric,

What a fool thing did I do to send you a bottle of champagne! I must have had a senior moment when I chose that gift as a token of my congratulations on your Oscar Golden Prize. I have intended to celebrate your hard working for the MGM film and you deserve it.

Please forgive my faux pas. Let's invite you to dinner. I will call you when I get back from Boston at the end of the week. I look forward to seeing you.

Yours sincerely,

Tony

亲爱的艾瑞克：

送你一瓶香槟做礼物真是太傻了！我真是一时糊涂才送这个礼物来庆祝你荣获奥斯卡金像奖。我的原意是想庆祝一下你为米高梅电影公司做的努力，而这也是你当之无愧的。

请原谅我的失礼，并让我请你吃顿午饭作为道歉。我这周末从波士顿回来后就前去拜访你。期待与你见面。

托尼

邮件回复 *Reply*

Dear Tony,

It's grateful of you to send me champagne though I don't really like it.

I love film and television career. I can achieve this success and honor, first of all due to the company's help and support, then to your help and encouragement in the low period of my career. I expect you come back to share my joy.

Yours,

Eric

亲爱的托尼：

虽然我不喜欢香槟酒，但是仍然很感谢你。

我热爱影视事业，我今天能取得这样的成就与荣誉，首先感谢公司对我事业的帮助与支持，其次也要感谢你在我事业的低谷时期对我的鼓舞与帮助。期待你回来与我一起分享我的喜悦。

艾瑞克

范例 17 | 因失言道歉

Dear Lily,

It is really difficult for me to write to you, because I know how embarrassed you were this morning for my impulsive statement. I feel very guilty and I should have been more aware of and sensitive to your feelings. While your timely help rescue, but my wayward words made you be in difficult situation.

I hope that you never mind my bad behaviors. I'll be sure to note the occasion of speech. Never again will I even think, much less make a remark like that.

I hope that you can forgive me from the bottom of your heart.

Yours sincerely,

Ellen

亲爱的莉莉：

提笔写下这封信真的很难，因为我知道，今天上午我的出言不逊让你多尴尬，我感到非常抱歉。我本应该考虑到你的感受。虽然你及时帮忙解围，但是我的任性却让你陷入困难的境地。

希望你不要介意我的胡言乱语。我以后一定会注意讲话的场合，绝不会再犯那样的错了，那样的话我连想都不会想。

希望你能打从心底原谅我。

埃伦 谨上

邮件回复 *Reply*

Dear Ellen,

I have seen your mail. I believe you do not mean to say that. Even though I am a little bit embarrassed but I can understand and sympathize with you. Moreover, it has been past and has not much effect on me. So you do not have to blame yourself. I hope such things will never happen again in the future.

Yours,

Lily

亲爱的埃伦：

我已经看到你的邮件了。我相信你并不是故意要那样讲的，所以尽管当时我有些尴尬，但我能理解并体谅你。况且事情已经过去也没有对我造成太大的影响，所以你也不用太过介意。相信以后也不会有这样的事发生。

莉莉

范例 18 | 因行为不妥道歉

Dear Xiao Min,

I want to apologize for my behavior at yesterday's birthday party. I am embarrassed about my bad argument, and hope that you never keep my behavior in your mind. If there is anything I can do to make up for my deficiency, I will do my every effort to reduce the impact on you.

I am very regretful for my crude behavior. I swear to you that I will pay more attention to my behavior, and take concrete actions to prove that such things will never happen the second time. I sincerely hope to have your forgiveness and expect this will not impair our friendship.

Yours sincerely,

Hua

亲爱的小敏：

我想为我昨晚生日派对上的行为向你道歉。事情发生后我感到很羞愧，并希望你不要放在心上。如果有什么可以补偿我的过失，我会尽一切努力减少对你的影响。

我对我粗鲁的行为感到很后悔。我向你保证以后我一定会注意我的行为，并以实际行动证明这样的事情绝对不会发生第二次。真心的希望能得到你的原谅并期望不会影响我们的友谊。

华 谨上

邮件回复 *Reply*

Dear Hua,

I have received your letter. From the letter I can see your self-blame and also feel your apology. I know who you are because we grew up together. Last night I think you were just drunk. I accept your apology and decide to forgive you. We are still friends. I think this incident will not affect our friendship.

Yours,

Xiao Min

亲爱的华：

你的邮件已收到，从信中我能看出你很自责，亦能感受到你的歉意。因为我们从小一起长大，我清楚你的为人，昨晚我相信你只是因为喝醉了的原因。我接受你的道歉并决定原谅你。我们是朋友，我想这件事不会影响我们的友谊。

小敏

范例 19 | 因招待不周道歉

Dear Robin,

It is a pity that I was not at home when you came to see me yesterday afternoon. The fact is that I had an engagement with some friends to accompany them to the cinema and I was ignorant of your visit. Not until nine o'clock in the evening did I come back. You must have been disappointed by my absence.

I hope you will stay one more week in this city. I will call on you on Tuesday morning at eight o'clock. Since this is the first time you come to Hangzhou, I will take you to visit some famous spots that you are expecting to. Please wait for me in your hotel at the appointed time.

Yours truly,

Jane

亲爱的罗宾：

非常抱歉，昨天下午让你的拜访落了空。事实是我与几个朋友事先有约，和他们一同去电影院了，因此将你的来访忘在脑后。直到晚上9点我才回来，我不在家你一定很失望吧。

希望这周你会继续停留本市一周。我会于周二早上8点钟拜访你。因为这是你第一次来杭州，我想带你参观一些你一直都想去的著名景点。请于约定的时间在酒店等我。

简

邮件回复 *Reply*

Dear Jane,

Seriously, I am sorry to hear that you are not at home. I wanted to discuss with you the gathering organized by the students. Your wife welcomed me very warmly. But I had something to deal with so I did not wait too long. You do not have to apologize for it. The work will last a period of time. I will be waiting for you on Tuesday.

Yours truly,

Robin

亲爱的简：

说真的你不在家真的有些遗憾，本来是想和你一起商量这次举办同学聚会的事情。不过您的太太很热情的接待了我，但是由于我有些事情要处理所以也没等太久，你也不必太过歉意。由于工作安排会继续停留一段时间，周二我会等你来。

罗宾

范例 20 | 因不辞而别道歉

Dear Kim,

I am writing to apologize for not saying goodbye to you. It was very impolite of me to do so especially as we have built good friendship.

Because, shortly after the visit, I received exciting news from my mother, saying that my wife had born a son ahead. I was so pleased at that news that I couldn't wait to return home to see my lovely son and great wife. I left so hurry that I forget to tell you. I feel terribly sorry for that.

To make up for my thoughtless behavior toward you, I want to invite you to come and stay with my family during the vacation. Please tell me as soon as you make a decision.

Yours sincerely,

Kevin

亲爱的金姆：

这封信是想表达我的歉意，我没向你告别便离开了。我真是非常失礼，尤其是我们的关系这么好。

因为，参观后不久，我从我母亲那收到了一个令人激动的消息，即我妻子提前生了个儿子。接到消息后我太高兴了，我迫不及待地要回去看看我可爱的儿子和伟大的妻子。我离开得太匆忙了以致来不及通知你。对此我感到非常抱歉。

为了弥补我对你的失礼行为，我想邀请你在假期到我家来，与我的家人一起待上一阵子。一旦决定请告诉我。

凯文

邮件回复 *Reply*

Dear Kevin,

What a happy day it is to witness a new born coming to the earth. We are old friends for many years, so I can understand your feelings. Please convey to your family my best wishes. I also hope the baby can grow up healthily and happily. This holiday I would go to see my cute nephew.

Yours sincerely,

Kim

亲爱的凯文：

这是个让人兴奋的消息，新生命的降临是件多么值得高兴的事，再说大家都是多年的老友，我很能理解你的心情。请向你的家人转达我的祝福，希望宝贝能够健康快乐地成长。这个假期我一定会亲自去看看我那可爱的侄子。

金姆

范例 21 | 因不能迎接道歉

Dear Diana,

I am eagerly expecting your visit to our city. Unfortunately, however, I regret to notify you that I will not be able to meet you at the airport timely.

The fact is that your flight will arrive early in the morning, and the earliest time I can arrive at the airport will be about 6:00 a.m. which will later an hour than you land. Will you please wait for me in the waiting lobby? You can have breakfast while you are waiting.

Hope we can meet soon.

Yours sincerely,

Danna

亲爱的戴安娜：

我非常期待你来我们城市观光旅游。但很遗憾，我抱歉地通知你我不能及时去机场接你了。

原因是你的飞机到达机场太早了，而我最早能赶到机场的时间是早上6点，这也要比你晚1小时后才能到。你可以在候机室等我吗？等待的这段时间你可以先吃早饭。

希望早点见到你。

丹娜 谨上

邮件回复 *Reply*

Dear Danna,

I am sorry that you have to pick me up so early. If it is not the first time to visit Wuhan, there is no need for you to pick me up so early. As you know, owing to the delay of the flight, I have to arrive Wuhan very early. This brings me a lot inconvenience. Of course, it also bothers you. I also hope to meet you soon.

Yours sincerely,

Diana

亲爱的丹娜：

对于那么早让你来接我我深表歉意，如果不是第一次来武汉我想一定不会让你这么辛苦的来接我。可你知道由于航班延误，我不得不很早就到武汉。这给我的出行带来了不便，当然也给你增添了不少麻烦。我也希望能够早点见到你。

戴安娜 谨上

范例 22 | 因遗失物品道歉

Dear Linda,

I am terribly sorry to tell you that I have lost the valuable encyclopedia book you lent me last week. I read it every day and intended to finish it quickly. Last night when I came to my room, I looked for it in every corner, but it hasn't been found. I will try to recover it as soon as possible. If I fail to find it, I will get a new book for you.

But I am afraid it can never take the place of the old one. For this irrecoverable loss, I should be to blame. I am so careless with my things. I will be more careful in the future.

Yours sincerely,

Bonnie

亲爱的琳达：

非常抱歉地告诉你，我弄丢了上星期你借给我的那本宝贵的百科全书。我每天都读，我打算很快看完它。昨晚我回到我的房间，到处都找不见那本书。我将尽力早日找到它，万一找不到，我只好买一本新书还给你。

但是，新书也不能取代那本旧书吧！这种不可弥补的损失，我应该受到责备。太粗心了。我以后一定要加倍小心。

邦尼 谨上

邮件回复 *Reply*

Dear Bonnie

I like the book very much. It is a birthday gift from my sister. So I hope you can find it. I think it is still in the room. Don't worry about that, if you can not find it. Please be careful next time. In addition, if you haven't finished reading this book, you can borrow one from the school library.

Yours sincerely,

Linda

亲爱的邦尼：

我很喜欢那本书的，是姐姐送我的生日礼物，所以我希望你能找到它。因为在房间里我想它是不会丢的。不过如果你实在找不到就算了，我知道你也不是故意弄丢的，以后小心就好。另外如果你还没读完这本书，你可以去图书馆借阅。

琳达 谨上

范例 23 | 因未及时退款道歉

Dear Tina,

Please allow me to apologize for missing your G&E refund check. I hope this hasn't brought too much inconvenience to you.

As you know, IEAD Intelligent Corporation is merging with the EDP Company. All the finance accounts are frozen from March 20, 2019. We will unfreeze these accounts within two weeks. So I will send your refund check before April 5, 2019. I apologize for the inconvenience on behalf of our company.

Once again, thank you for your understanding in this matter.

Yours sincerely,

Rita

亲爱的蒂娜：

请允许我对于漏掉了你的G&E退款支票表示深深的歉意。我希望这没有给你带来太多不便。

如你所知，IEAD智能集团正在与EDP公司进行合并。2019年3月20日开始，所有账户都已冻结，两周之后才能解冻。因此，我将于2019年4月5日之前把你的退款支票寄给你。我代表公司对于由此给你带来的不便表示道歉。

再一次感谢你对这件事情的理解。

瑞塔 谨上

邮件回复 *Reply*

Dear Rita,

I am angry because your behavior caused lot losses to us, which greatly influences our work. I hope this won't happen again. Even though something like this happens, you should notify us as soon as possible. We can do some preparations. Please send the refund check to us quickly.

Wish you all the best!

Yours sincerely,

Tina

亲爱的瑞塔：

我为你们给我造成的损失表示愤慨。这种延迟耽误了我很多的工作。我希望下次不要出现这样的情况。即使有类似的事情也要及时地通知我们，方便我们做相应的调整。请尽快把退款支票邮寄给我们。

祝好！

蒂娜 谨上

范例 24｜因爱莫能助道歉

Dear Pat,

I must apologize for not being able to help you when you asked me to recommend you to the director of the Hospital Attached to Capital Medical University.

Unfortunately, I haven't seen Jim Green, Director of the Hospital Attached to Capital Medical University for a long time and I had no chance of mentioning you to him.

I make sure that I will mention you if I happen to bump into him. I hope you will do well in your research work.

Yours sincerely,

Douglas

亲爱的帕特：

很抱歉你曾让我向首都医科大学附属医院的主任推荐你，但一直没有帮上忙。

不巧的是我已经很长时间没有见到首都医科大学附属医院的主任吉姆·格林了。我一直没有机会向他提及你。

如果我有机会碰见他我一定向他介绍你，希望你在研究工作中一切顺利。

道格拉斯 谨上

邮件回复 *Reply*

Dear Douglas,

I have paid a visit to him privately. He said he missed you very much. We have exchanged many thoughts happily. We also discussed many question in our major. He is a very nice person and very talkative. He helped me solve many doubts which I couldn't understand. I believe that we could cooperate well in the future.

Wish everything goes well with your work.

Yours sincerely,

Pat

亲爱的道格拉斯：

我已经私下里拜访了他。他说他也很想念你。我们在一起交流得很愉快。我们探讨了很多有关自己专业的问题。他是一个很和蔼的人，而且很健谈。他替我解决了很多我一直都没有弄明白的问题。相信我们在未来可以很好地合作。

祝你一切都好！

帕特 谨上

范例 25 | 因未回信道歉

Dear Daisy,

Please forgive me for not having answered your letter of November 10. If I tell you the reason, I believe that you will understand me. When your letter arrived, I was just in Macau. As my family could not forward it to me during my absence, it has been, therefore, lying in my room until the moment I took it up. I am really sorry for not informing you timely.

I enjoyed many pleasant sights during my travel. I shall be pleased to give you an account of them when I see you next time.

Yours sincerely,

Ruby

亲爱的黛西：

请原谅我收到你11月10日的来信后迟迟未回复，如果我告诉你原因，相信你一定会理解我的。收到你的信时，我正巧身在澳门，家人不方便转寄。你的信一直放在我房间里，直到我回来才看见，我真的很抱歉没有及时通知你。

这次出去旅行让我饱览了许多怡人的风光，下次见到你时，我会给你讲述我的旅游经历。

露比

邮件回复 *Reply*

Dear Ruby,

Don't be sorry for this. I know that you are always very busy. The last letter I wrote is just to say hello to you. From your letter, I know you have been to Macau. I also want to have a visit of Macao, but I don't have time. I am very pleased that if you can show me your photos in Macau. I expect you will tell me your experience of your travel. Hope to see you soon.

Wish you and your family all the best!

Yours sincerely,

Daisy

亲爱的露比：

不用为此而感到抱歉。我知道你一直都很忙。上次写信只是向你问好。从你的来信，我知道你去了澳门了。我很想到澳门去，但一直没有时间去。如果你能把你在那里的照片给我看，我将不胜感激。我也很期待你给我讲你的旅游经历。真的很希望早点见到你。

祝你和家人都好！

黛西 谨上

范例 26 | 打扰某人的致歉

Dear Antony,

I am writing this letter to apologize to you. I feel really sorry to call you so late last night to ask you about the contract. Because yesterday I found that there is something wrong in contract which needs to be modified as soon as possible.You are the person in charge, so I had to call you so late.

I'm very sorry to bother you. I hope you can forgive me.

Yours sincerely,

Adam

亲爱的安东尼：

我写这封信是为了向你道歉。昨天晚上那么晚打电话给你询问你有关合约的事情，实在很抱歉。由于昨天才发现合约里的那个部分有些问题需要马上修改。而你是主要负责人，我只能在那么晚打电话给你。

非常抱歉打扰你的正常休息。希望你见谅。

亚当 谨上

邮件回复 *Reply*

Dear Adam

Don't mind about this. I think I should thank your timely warning that there was something wrong in the contract, to help me avoid causing loss.

Best wishes!

Yours sincerely,

Antony

亲爱的亚当：

不要把这件事情放在心上。这件事还要多谢你及时发现了合约里存在的问题，以避免发生损失。

祝好！

安东尼 谨上

范例 27｜错怪某人的致歉

Dear Antony,

I'm sorry I blamed you on broking my bike. Because I saw my bike had already broken when you pushed it yesterday, I thought you were the person who should be in charge of this. And I also called your name very loudly. But then I knew this was not your fault, and in fact you were the person who wanted to help to repair the broken bike. I think I should apologize for my bad temper.

Please accept my sincere apology for doing that.

Yours sincerely,

Adam

亲爱的安东尼：

我很抱歉错怪你弄坏了我的自行车。因为昨天我看见你推着我的车的时候它已经坏了，所以我就认为是你把它弄坏的，还很大声的骂你。但是后来我才知道，原来你是要帮我修理已经坏掉的自行车。我想我应该为我的坏脾气道歉。

请你接受我真挚的歉意。

亚当 谨上

邮件回复 *Reply*

Dear Adam,

I am not angry with you. I know you very well. This bike is your treasure. So I know why you was so angry with me. Never mind. I will forget what you said yesterday.

Best wishes!

Yours sincerely,

Antony

亲爱的亚当：

我没有生气。我了解你，这辆自行车是你的宝贝。也难怪你会这么生气。你不用介意。我没有把你的话放在心上。

祝好！

安东尼 谨上